MICROSOFT
OUTLOOK® 98
FOR WINDOWS® FOR
DUMMIES®

Quick Reference

by Bill Dyszel

IDG
BOOKS
WORLDWIDE

IDG Books Worldwide, Inc.
An International Data Group Company

Foster City, CA ✦ Chicago, IL ✦ Indianapolis, IN ✦ New York, NY

Microsoft® Outlook® 98 For Windows® For Dummies® Quick Reference

Published by
IDG Books Worldwide, Inc.
An International Data Group Company
919 E. Hillsdale Blvd.
Suite 400
Foster City, CA 94404
www.idgbooks.com (IDG Books Worldwide Web site)
www.dummies.com (Dummies Press Web site)

Library of Congress Catalog Card No.: 98-85430

ISBN: 0-7645-0394-4

Printed in the United States of America

10 9 8 7 6 5 4

1P/SW/QV/QQ/IN

Distributed in the United States by IDG Books Worldwide, Inc.

Distributed by CDG Books Canada Inc. for Canada; by Transworld Publishers Limited in the United Kingdom; by IDG Norge Books for Norway; by IDG Sweden Books for Sweden; by IDG Books Australia Publishing Corporation Pty. Ltd. for Australia and New Zealand; by TransQuest Publishers Pte Ltd. for Singapore, Malaysia, Thailand, Indonesia, and Hong Kong; by Gotop Information Inc. for Taiwan; by ICG Muse, Inc. for Japan; by Intersoft for South Africa; by Eyrolles for France; by International Thomson Publishing for Germany, Austria and Switzerland; by Distribuidora Cuspide for Argentina; by LR International for Brazil; by Galileo Libros for Chile; by Ediciones ZETA S.C.R. Ltda. for Peru; by WS Computer Publishing Corporation, Inc., for the Philippines; by Contemporanea de Ediciones for Venezuela; by Express Computer Distributors for the Caribbean and West Indies; by Micronesia Media Distributor, Inc. for Micronesia; by Chips Computadoras S.A. de C.V. for Mexico; by Editorial Norma de Panama S.A. for Panama; by American Bookshops for Finland.

For general information on IDG Books Worldwide's books in the U.S., please call our Consumer Customer Service department at 800-762-2974. For reseller information, including discounts and premium sales, please call our Reseller Customer Service department at 800-434-3422.

For information on where to purchase IDG Books Worldwide's books outside the U.S., please contact our International Sales department at 317-596-5530 or fax 317-572-4002.

For consumer information on foreign language translations, please contact our Customer Service department at 1-800-434-3422, fax 317-572-4002, or e-mail rights@idgbooks.com.

For information on licensing foreign or domestic rights, please phone +1-650-653-7098.

For sales inquiries and special prices for bulk quantities, please contact our Order Services department at 800-434-3422 or write to the address above.

For information on using IDG Books Worldwide's books in the classroom or for ordering examination copies, please contact our Educational Sales department at 800-434-2086 or fax 317-572-4005.

For press review copies, author interviews, or other publicity information, please contact our Public Relations department at 650-653-7000 or fax 650-653-7500.

For authorization to photocopy items for corporate, personal, or educational use, please contact Copyright Clearance Center, 222 Rosewood Drive, Danvers, MA 01923, or fax 978-750-4470.

is a trademark under exclusive license to IDG Books Worldwide, Inc., from International Data Group, Inc.

About the Author

Bill Dyszel writes frequently for leading computer magazines, including *PC Magazine, Windows Sources,* and *Computer Shopper,* while also working as a consultant to many of New York's leading firms in the securities, advertising, and publishing industries. His list of current and former clients includes Salomon Brothers, First Boston, Goldman Sachs, Ogilvy & Mather, KMPG Peat Marwick, and many others. He is currently preparing to write a book on his favorite gadget, the PalmPilot handheld computer.

The world of high technology has led Bill to grapple with such subjects as multimedia (or how to make your $2,000 computer do the work of a $20 radio), personal information managers (how to make your $3,000 laptop computer do the work of a $3 date book), and graphics programs (how to make your $5,000 package of computers and peripheral devices do the work of a 50-cent box of crayons). All joking aside, he has found that after you've figured out the process, most of this stuff can be useful, helpful, and, yes, even cool. He elaborates on that idea on his Web site (www.pcstudio.com) and in his speeches and seminars about making technology fun. He'll even send you his occasional e-mail newsletter about the things he finds enjoyable and useful; just drop a note to his e-mail address (BillDyszel@pcstudio.com).

Like many public figures with skeletons in their closets, this author has a secret past. Before entering the computer industry, Bill sang with the New York City Opera and worked regularly on the New York stage as a singer, actor, and writer in numerous plays, musicals, and operas. His opera spoof, *99% ARTFREE!,* won critical praise from *The New York Times,* the New York *Daily News,* and the Associated Press when he performed the show off-Broadway.

ABOUT IDG BOOKS WORLDWIDE

Welcome to the world of IDG Books Worldwide.

IDG Books Worldwide, Inc., is a subsidiary of International Data Group, the world's largest publisher of computer-related information and the leading global provider of information services on information technology. IDG was founded more than 30 years ago by Patrick J. McGovern and now employs more than 9,000 people worldwide. IDG publishes more than 290 computer publications in over 75 countries. More than 90 million people read one or more IDG publications each month.

Launched in 1990, IDG Books Worldwide is today the #1 publisher of best-selling computer books in the United States. We are proud to have received eight awards from the Computer Press Association in recognition of editorial excellence and three from Computer Currents' First Annual Readers' Choice Awards. Our best-selling ...For Dummies® series has more than 50 million copies in print with translations in 31 languages. IDG Books Worldwide, through a joint venture with IDG's Hi-Tech Beijing, became the first U.S. publisher to publish a computer book in the People's Republic of China. In record time, IDG Books Worldwide has become the first choice for millions of readers around the world who want to learn how to better manage their businesses.

Our mission is simple: Every one of our books is designed to bring extra value and skill-building instructions to the reader. Our books are written by experts who understand and care about our readers. The knowledge base of our editorial staff comes from years of experience in publishing, education, and journalism — experience we use to produce books to carry us into the new millennium. In short, we care about books, so we attract the best people. We devote special attention to details such as audience, interior design, use of icons, and illustrations. And because we use an efficient process of authoring, editing, and desktop publishing our books electronically, we can spend more time ensuring superior content and less time on the technicalities of making books.

You can count on our commitment to deliver high-quality books at competitive prices on topics you want to read about. At IDG Books Worldwide, we continue in the IDG tradition of delivering quality for more than 30 years. You'll find no better book on a subject than one from IDG Books Worldwide.

John Kilcullen
Chairman and CEO
IDG Books Worldwide, Inc.

WINNER
Eighth Annual Computer Press Awards ≥1992

WINNER
Ninth Annual Computer Press Awards ≥1993

WINNER
Tenth Annual Computer Press Awards ≥1994

WINNER
Eleventh Annual Computer Press Awards ≥1995

IDG is the world's leading IT media, research and exposition company. Founded in 1964, IDG had 1997 revenues of $2.05 billion and has more than 9,000 employees worldwide. IDG offers the widest range of media options that reach IT buyers in 75 countries representing 95% of worldwide IT spending. IDG's diverse product and services portfolio spans six key areas including print publishing, online publishing, expositions and conferences, market research, education and training, and global marketing services. More than 90 million people read one or more of IDG's 290 magazines and newspapers, including IDG's leading global brands — Computerworld, PC World, Network World, Macworld and the Channel World family of publications. IDG Books Worldwide is one of the fastest-growing computer book publishers in the world, with more than 700 titles in 36 languages. The "...For Dummies®" series alone has more than 50 million copies in print. IDG offers online users the largest network of technology-specific Web sites around the world through IDG.net (http://www.idg.net), which comprises more than 225 targeted Web sites in 55 countries worldwide. International Data Corporation (IDC) is the world's largest provider of information technology data, analysis and consulting, with research centers in over 41 countries and more than 400 research analysts worldwide. IDG World Expo is a leading producer of more than 168 globally branded conferences and expositions in 35 countries including E3 (Electronic Entertainment Expo), Macworld Expo, ComNet, Windows World Expo, ICE (Internet Commerce Expo), Agenda, DEMO, and Spotlight. IDG's training subsidiary, ExecuTrain, is the world's largest computer training company, with more than 230 locations worldwide and 785 training courses. IDG Marketing Services helps industry-leading IT companies build international brand recognition by developing global integrated marketing programs via IDG's print, online and exposition products worldwide. Further information about the company can be found at www.idg.com. 1/26/00

Author's Acknowledgments

I'd like to thank all the wonderful people who helped me make this book entertaining and useful to the reader, especially Greg Robertson, Mike Zulich, Mike Kelly, Mary Corder, Mary Bednarek, Diane Steele, Darlene Wong, and the whole staff of IDG Books Worldwide, who make this series possible.

Thanks to my friends, editors, and colleagues at *Windows Sources* magazine, *Computer Shopper,* and *PC Magazine.* Thanks to the people at Microsoft and Waggener Edstrom, who also helped me figure things out, especially Rob Price. Above all, thanks to my personal cheering section, led by Leigh Williams.

Publisher's Acknowledgments

We're proud of this book; please register your comments through our IDG Books Worldwide Online Registration Form located at http://my2cents.dummies.com.

Some of the people who helped bring this book to market include the following:

Acquisitions, Editorial, and Media Development

Project Editor: Gregory R. Robertson

Aquisitions Manager: Michael Kelly

Technical Editor: Michael Zulich

Editorial Manager: Mary C. Corder

Editorial Assistant: Michael D. Sullivan

Production

Associate Project Coordinator: Tom Missler

Layout and Graphics: Lou Boudreau, J. Tyler Connor, Maridee V. Ennis, Angela F. Hunckler, Drew R. Moore, Brent Savage, Dan Whetstine

Proofreaders: Kelli Botta, Michelle Croninger, Kathleen Sparrow

Indexer: Sherry Massey

Special Help
Suzanne Thomas, Associate Editor

General and Administrative

IDG Books Worldwide, Inc.: John Kilcullen, CEO

IDG Books Technology Publishing Group: Richard Swadley, Senior Vice President and Publisher; Walter R. Bruce III, Vice President and Publisher; Joseph Wikert, Vice President and Publisher; Mary Bednarek, Vice President and Director, Product Development; Andy Cummings, Publishing Director, General User Group; Mary C. Corder, Editorial Director; Barry Pruett, Publishing Director

IDG Books Consumer Publishing Group: Roland Elgey, Senior Vice President and Publisher; Kathleen A. Welton, Vice President and Publisher; Kevin Thornton, Acquisitions Manager; Kristin A. Cocks, Editorial Director

IDG Books Internet Publishing Group: Brenda McLaughlin, Senior Vice President and Publisher; Sofia Marchant, Online Marketing Manager

IDG Books Production for Branded Press: Debbie Stailey, Director of Production; Cindy L. Phipps, Manager of Project Coordination, Production Proofreading, and Indexing; Tony Augsburger, Manager of Prepress, Reprints, and Systems; Laura Carpenter, Production Control Manager; Shelley Lea, Supervisor of Graphics and Design; Debbie J. Gates, Production Systems Specialist; Robert Springer, Supervisor of Proofreading; Kathie Schutte, Production Supervisor

Packaging and Book Design: Patty Page, Manager, Promotions Marketing

♦

The publisher would like to give special thanks to Patrick J. McGovern, without whom this book would not have been possible.

♦

Contents at a Glance

Table of Contents

Part III: The Calendar 63

Part IV: Tasks 87

How to Use This Book

Welcome to *Microsoft Outlook 98 For Windows For Dummies Quick Reference,* the compact, travel-sized version of the full-strength *Microsoft Outlook 98 For Windows For Dummies.*

As they say on *Dragnet,* this book is "Just the facts, ma'am." I'll just tell you how to do what you need to do in Outlook and leave out the details about why. For more elaborate explanations of the whys and wherefores of Outlook, check out the companion volume, *Microsoft Outlook 98 For Windows For Dummies.*

How This Book Is Organized

You won't find out everything you need to know about Microsoft Outlook from this one skinny volume. That's why I wrote a fat, friendly volume called *Microsoft Outlook 98 For Windows For Dummies.* If you can't decide between this light, low-fat version and the other, authoritative, luxury version, I recommend keeping things simple and getting both. (I like to be helpful.)

This book is organized alphabetically by task so that you can easily find information by browsing through the sections or by looking in the index or table of contents.

Outlook is simple enough to use, and many different tasks are done with the same tools, so you'll probably pick it up pretty quickly. With a little help from this book on where to begin and how to get started, you can find your way without much fuss.

What's in This Book

This book contains seven parts and a glossary.

Part I: All about Outlook

Outlook works differently than some of the other Microsoft programs, but after you get a handle on what the different parts of the Outlook screen can do, you'll catch on fast. I also include instructions for using a few of the more interesting — and free! — specialized applications that you can access from the Microsoft Web site. I tried them and found using them fun, but frustrating at first. These tips should save you the frustration.

Part II: E-Mail

E-mail is quick and easy, and Outlook can make it easier. This part shows you the nitty-gritty details of exchanging messages with individuals or groups and using the features of Outlook that make e-mail such an efficient business tool.

Part III: The Calendar

If time is money, your calendar should make you rich, right? This section gives you the basic rundown on the tools that Outlook offers to help you manage your time; for managing money, you're on your own.

Part IV: Tasks

When you do that voodoo that you do so well, you may want to keep a list of things to do (your Voodoo To Do); just to be sure that the things you wanted to do got done. I'll show you how to use Outlook for managing your tasks with a minimum of Black Magic.

Part V: Contacts

If you're exchanging e-mail and keeping a calendar of appointments, I assume other people are involved. (Otherwise, look for my upcoming book *Microsoft Outlook For Hermits*.) The Contacts section covers Outlook's tools for keeping track of names, addresses, phone numbers, e-mail addresses, and general stuff.

Part VI: Notes and Journal

Outlook enables you to create handy little notes to jog your memory, and even keeps a running chronological record of every document you create — in case you forgot to remember in the first place. This section describes how to deal with two odd but useful features of Outlook.

Part VII: Files and Folders

This section tells you how to use Outlook's rather facile facilities for dealing with files, folders, and all the other stuff on your computer.

Conventions Used in This Book

To keep this book brief and to the point, I'll assume that you're comfortable with Windows 95 and Microsoft Office. If you're new to those packages, I strongly recommend the appropriate *...For Dummies* books on those programs.

I'm a confessed keyboard freak, so I prefer to show you keyboard shortcuts wherever possible. When you see

Ctrl+Z

that means press the Ctrl key and the letter Z at the same time. When you see

File⟹Open

that means click your mouse on the word File in the menu bar and then click the Open command. The underlined letters are *hot keys,* which enable you to keep your hands on the keyboard. You can use the hot keys to open the File menu by holding down the Alt key and the letter F at the same time, and then releasing both keys and choosing the Open command by pressing the letter O.

What the Pictures Mean

I've sprinkled icons throughout this book to make things so clear that you really don't need me to explain them. Of course, that won't stop me from explaining them anyway.

This is a tip to save you time or effort.

This icon alerts you to a problem to avoid.

This shows you the quickest way to do something.

This icon points out a feature of the program that seems nonsensical — because it *is* nonsensical.

This points you to a more complete explanation in the full-sized, luxury edition of *Microsoft Outlook 98 For Windows For Dummies.*

This icon points to a feature that requires you to be networked through Microsoft Exchange Server in order to take advantage of it.

Other Stuff

Microsoft Outlook gives you the tools you need for real desktop productivity: You easily can use each module without leaving your other Office applications when needed. And Microsoft plans more features in the future. At least you know there's more to Outlook than meets the eye. This book will help you discover more of it.

All about Outlook

Outlook offers you a lot more than would fit in this itty-bitty volume. I'm going to stick to the important stuff, so you can leap right in and start making Outlook a valuable tool in your daily work.

The Outlook functions that are immediately useful are the Personal Information Management features. These features show up as soon as you start the program. Microsoft cleverly designed Outlook to enable you to program and customize it to do almost anything you want that involves managing data. Some of the tasks that Outlook plans to do for you in the future are still a gleam in some programmer's eye, such as storing voice mail messages and advanced fax services. In the meantime, I focus on what Outlook offers here and now.

In this part . . .

- ✔ **About the screen**
- ✔ **Drag and drop**
- ✔ **Microsoft Exchange Server**
- ✔ **Microsoft Office and Outlook**
- ✔ **Options**
- ✔ **Specialized applications**

About the Screen

After you start Outlook, you see a screen within a screen. The area along the top edge and the left side of the screen offers you a collection of menus and icons. These menus and icons enable you to control what you see and what you make happen in the remainder of the screen. The different parts of the Outlook screen have names:

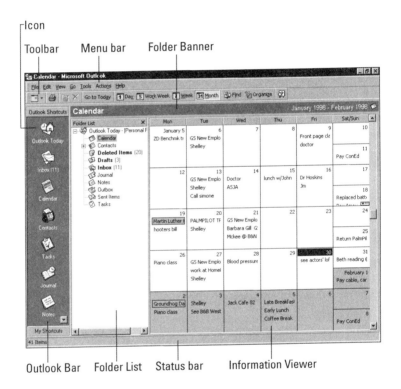

Icon

Toolbar   Menu bar   Folder Banner

Outlook Bar   Folder List   Status bar   Information Viewer

The Outlook Bar

Running along the left side of the Outlook screen is the Outlook Bar. The Outlook Bar contains large, clearly marked icons for each of the Outlook modules: Outlook Today, Inbox, Calendar, Contacts, Tasks, Journal, Notes, and Deleted Items. You can click any icon at any time to switch to a different module and then switch back, just like changing channels on your TV.

The Outlook Bar also has three gray separator bars, named Outlook Shortcuts, My Shortcuts, and Other Shortcuts. You can click these separator bars to switch to a different section of the

Outlook Bar that has a different set of icons. You can add icons to any section of the Outlook Bar. You can also add sections to the bar itself by right-clicking the Outlook Bar. This action opens the shortcut menu, which enables you to choose the appropriate command.

The Folder Banner

The Folder Banner is the name of the area that sits below the toolbars and above the main part of the Outlook screen (known as the Information Viewer). The name of the folder or module you're using is displayed in large letters at the left end of the Folder Banner. The right end of the banner displays a large icon. This icon is also used by the Outlook Bar to represent the module you're using.

Other information also turns up from time to time in the Folder Banner, such as the following:

✦ The alphabetical section of the Contact list you're currently viewing

✦ Whether you're using something called *filtering,* which enables you to limit the information displayed on the screen to items that meet certain criteria (see "Filtering" in Part V)

✦ The Group By Box when you're using grouped views (see "Using grouped views" in Part V)

In addition, clicking the triangle next to the name of the module or folder on the left end of the Folder Banner reveals a copy of the Folder List.

The Folder List

The Folder List gives you a quick peek behind the scenes at what's going on in Outlook. I leave the Folder List closed most of the time. If you're interested, however, here's what goes on behind the scenes.

Outlook organizes all the information you enter into folders. Each Outlook module has its own folder. Although you usually change modules by clicking the icon for that module in the Outlook Bar, you can also switch to a different module by clicking the folder for that module in the Folder List. Every Outlook module that has an icon in the Outlook Bar has a folder in the Folder List, but not every folder in the Folder List is represented by an icon in the Outlook Bar. Because you can have more folders in the Folder List than icons in the Outlook Bar, you may need to use the Folder List to go to a specific folder rather than click its icon in the Outlook Bar.

To open the Folder List, choose View⇨Folder List from the menu bar. The Folder List takes up so much space on the screen that I really can't do much work. That's why I leave it closed most of the time.

The Information Viewer

The biggest part of the Outlook screen, on the lower-right side, is the Information Viewer. Whatever you ask Outlook to show you shows up in the Information Viewer. Dates in your Calendar, messages in your Inbox, and names in your Contact list all appear in the Information Viewer.

You can drag items out of the Information Viewer to icons on the Outlook Bar to create new types of Outlook items from the information you already have (see "Drag and Drop" later in this part).

Menus

Like all Windows programs, Outlook has a menu bar across the top of the screen. Click your mouse on a menu name, such as File, Edit, or View, to make a menu of commands appear. The underlined letter in a menu name is a hot key; holding down the Alt key while pressing that letter does the same thing as clicking the mouse on the menu name.

On-screen forms

Each time you either open an item or create a new item in Outlook, a form appears. This form either accepts the information you want to enter or contains the information that you're viewing — or both. Each module has its own form, and each form has its own menus and toolbars.

You can also create your own forms with Outlook, or you can download new collections of forms from the Internet. For more about customizing Outlook forms, see *Microsoft Outlook 98 For Windows For Dummies* by yours truly (IDG Books Worldwide, Inc.).

Status bar

The gray bar across the bottom of the Outlook screen is the status bar, which tells you how many items are currently displayed and a few other pieces of essential information.

Toolbars

Toolbars offer a quicker way to control Outlook than clicking menus. The Outlook toolbar changes as you switch between different modules or views, to offer you the most useful set of tools for the task you're doing at the moment. If you see a tool and want to know what it does, let your mouse pointer hover over the tool but don't click; a ToolTip box appears, revealing the name of the tool. Outlook 98 has two toolbars that you can choose from on the main screen, the Standard toolbar and the Advanced toolbar. The Advanced toolbar offers you a larger selection of tools. You can pick the toolbar you want to use by choosing View⇨Toolbars and clicking the name of the toolbar you want to see.

Drag and Drop

You can do a surprising amount of work without ever touching the keyboard. That little old mouse of yours can drag items from one part of Outlook and drop them onto the icons in the Outlook Bar to create new items. After you drop an item from one Outlook module into another, Outlook transforms the information and makes the item useful in a whole new way: An e-mail message can become a Contact item, for example, or a Contact item can become a Journal entry, and so on.

Contact records created from e-mail messages

If someone sends you an e-mail message, you have all the information you need to create a new Contact record and enter that person in your Contact list.

To create a new Contact record, follow these steps:

1. Click the Inbox icon to see your current incoming messages.

2. Click a message from a person whose name you want to add to your Contact list and then drag it to the Contacts icon to open a New Contact form.

3. Enter whatever information you want to enter other than the
e-mail address (which is already there) in the appropriate text
boxes (see Part V for more information).

4. Click Save and Close (or press Alt+S).

A new contact is now part of your Contact list. Although you can
drag any type of item to the Contacts icon, e-mail messages are the
only items that make sense to drag there. Doing so saves you time
by providing information that you need in a Contact record
anyway.

E-mail messages created from appointments

You can send an e-mail message informing someone of an existing
appointment or inviting someone to attend a meeting. The person
to whom you're sending the message gets an e-mail message, with
the particulars of the appointment serving as the body of the
message.

To send an e-mail message with information about an appointment, follow these steps:

1. Click the Calendar icon to open your list of appointments.

2. Drag an appointment to the Inbox icon to open a New Message
form with details of the appointment filled in.

3. Fill in the e-mail address of the person to whom you want to send notice of the appointment, as well as any other information you want to include (see Part III for more about appointments).

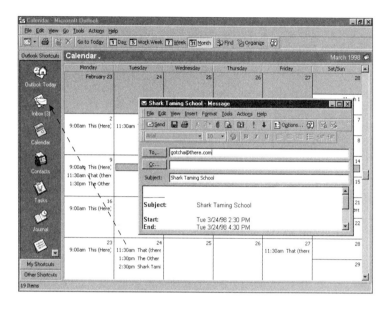

4. Click Send (or press Alt+S).

If you and anyone you're inviting to the meeting are using a computer connected to a network that uses Microsoft Exchange Server, you can click the Meeting Planner tab on the Appointment form to check their schedules before calling the meeting. If you're not using Exchange Server, e-mail is your best bet for inviting others to attend your meeting or appointment.

E-mail messages created from your Contact list

If you've already entered a person's e-mail address in your Contact list, you have all you need to create an e-mail message for that person.

1. Click the Contacts icon to open the Contact list.

2. Drag the name of the person to whom you're sending a message to the Inbox icon. A New Message form opens with the contact's address already filled in.

3. Enter whatever other information you want in the appropriate text boxes (see Part II for more about e-mail).

4. Click Send (or press Alt+S).

If you send your e-mail over an online service or the Internet, clicking Send only sends your message to the Outbox. To deliver your message to your recipient via your online service or Internet service provider (ISP), you have to press F5.

If you're on an office network using Exchange Server, clicking Send sends your message directly to the recipient.

Journal entries created from a Contact record

You can create a Journal entry from any name in your Contact list. Use drag and drop to create a Journal entry with a link to the contact. Drag and drop goes beyond saving you the effort of entering contact information in the New Journal Entry form. You can hop right to the Contact record from the Journal entry to find the contact's address, phone number, or other information.

To find a Contact record from a Journal entry, follow these steps:

1. Click the Contacts icon to open the Contact list.

2. Drag the name of the contact from the Contact list to the Journal icon in the Outlook Bar to open a New Journal Entry form.

3. Choose the type of Journal entry from the Entry Type list box. You can make a Journal entry for a letter, conversation, phone call, e-mail, or any of the 20-odd choices available in the Entry Type list box. I like to make Journal entries of incoming phone calls.

4. Fill in any other information in the appropriate text box.

5. Click Save and Close (or press Alt+S).

Your new entry is recorded in the Journal.

You can set up Outlook to make automatic Journal entries for new documents, e-mail messages, and AutoDialed phone calls. This automatic entry means that you don't need to create additional Journal entries for those events (see Part VI for more about the Journal).

Text exchange with other Windows programs

I like to save snippets from various documents and Web pages to my collection of notes for later reference. The process of dragging text from other applications is easier to do than to explain, so bear with me.

To save text from other applications, follow these steps:

1. Select the information you want to save by dragging your mouse over the desired text. Your text is highlighted to show what you've selected.

2. Hold down the Ctrl key while dragging the information from the original program down to the Outlook icon on the Windows 95 Taskbar at the bottom of the screen. (The Outlook icon says Inbox, Notes, or whatever Outlook module you're using at the time.)

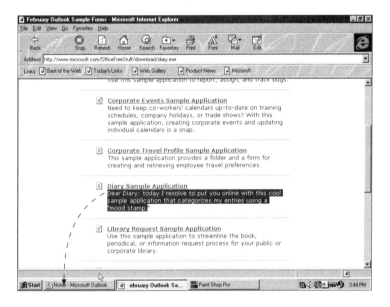

3. Hold the mouse on the Outlook icon without releasing the mouse button for a second or so, while Outlook appears.

4. After Outlook appears, drag the mouse pointer over to the Notes icon (or any icon in the Outlook bar) and release the mouse button to see the note on your screen.

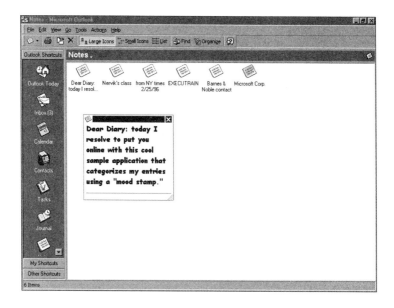

5. When your text appears in a note, press Esc to close the note.

You can actually drag text to any Outlook module, but Notes is the most useful module to drag things into. In other modules, the text always ends up in the box at the bottom of the New Item form. You can always select and drag text up from the box at the bottom of the form after you've captured the information in the form.

Undeleting deleted items

You can delete any Outlook item by dragging the item to the Deleted Items icon on the Outlook Bar. I won't go into detail about how to drag items to the Deleted Items folder.

Clicking the item you want to delete and then clicking the Delete button on the toolbar or pressing the Delete key on your keyboard is a whole bunch easier.

Undeleting items by dragging them out of the Deleted Items folder is just as simple and more useful when you have the need.

To undelete deleted items, follow these steps:

1. Click the Deleted Items icon in the Outlook Bar to open the list of deleted items.

2. Drag the deleted item that you want to restore back to the icon of the module from which the item came (contacts to the Contacts icon, tasks to the Tasks icon, and so on).

After you drag an item from the Deleted Items folder back to the folder from which it came, the item takes its place among all the other items in the folder, as if it had never been deleted.

Microsoft Exchange Server

If you use Outlook at an office connected to a network, you may have certain features that stand-alone (non-networked) Outlook users don't enjoy. The most important network features are available only if the network you're connected to uses a product called Microsoft Exchange Server. Exchange Server adds features, such as shared folders and custom applications for special needs. I don't go into depth to explain Exchange Server in this book. The following sections, however, show how you can use important features that you may encounter if you're using both Outlook and Microsoft Exchange Server.

Public Folders

In its simplest form, a Public Folder consists of a folder full of Outlook items that a large number of people can read and add to as they want. With the Public Folder, you can conduct conversations with a group of people more easily than by sending an e-mail message to everybody in a large group.

Here's how to take advantage of Public Folders if they are available to you:

1. Click the Folder List button on the toolbar to open the Folder List.

2. Click the name of the folder you want to see. A list of the items in the folder appears in the Information Viewer.

3. Double-click the name of any item that you want to read, in order to open the Discussion Item form.

4. If you want to read the next item, click the Next Item button in the form toolbar or press Ctrl+>. The next item in the folder appears.

5. If you want to reply to an item you read, click the Reply button in the Outlook Bar; then enter your response and click Post to add your message to the other messages in the folder.

You can create Public Folders for any reason at all. You may have a Public Folder dedicated to conducting business discussions, making personal announcements, offering classified ads, or whatever.

One of the most confusing aspects of Outlook is the fact that Microsoft assumes that everyone using Outlook is also using Microsoft Exchange Server. Many Outlook menus have commands that you can't use at all without Exchange Server. And you have to dig pretty deep into the Outlook Help files to figure out which features require Exchange Server and which ones don't. Some features work whether or not you have Exchange Server, but they behave differently in different situations. Obviously, Microsoft wants everyone to use Outlook *and* Microsoft Exchange Server. In this book I'm assuming that you're *not* using Exchange Server; when Exchange Server is specifically required, I tell you.

Some other features of Microsoft Exchange Server

If you're one of the fortunate few using Outlook on a network with Microsoft Exchange Server, you can do some useful things with Outlook that non-networked users can't do, such as the following:

✦ **Read Internet newsgroups:** If your network administrator sees fit, you can read Internet newsgroups through Outlook and Exchange Server. Internet *newsgroups* are places where people all over the world can post messages about various subjects, and others can respond to those messages with messages of their own. Newsgroups are a lot like the Public Folders I describe in the preceding section, except that newsgroups are open to everybody on the Internet, whereas Public Folders are more likely to be restricted to use by people at the company you work for. Each Internet newsgroup is organized to serve people who are interested in a specific topic. Tens of thousands of newsgroups exist, devoted to discussions about topics as varied as cooking, dogs, movie stars, and, of course, nearly every type of computer software. Microsoft has been making noises about giving non-networked Outlook users the capability to read Internet newsgroups in the "very near future." Microsoft's definition of the "very near future" can mean anything from two weeks to never, so you'll have to wait and see.

✦ **Share your calendar with others:** Scheduling a meeting with others in your organization is easier when you know who's available when. With Microsoft Exchange Server, you can look at the calendar of each individual and find a time when all of you are free and then schedule the meeting accordingly. Outlook 98 has a feature called Net Folders, which also enables you to share calendar information with any other Outlook 98 user via e-mail. If you use Net Folders, you don't absolutely need Exchange to share calendars, but Exchange does the job more efficiently.

✦ **Synchronize offline folders:** Both Microsoft Exchange Server and Outlook organize information into folders, but Outlook stores the folders on your computer, whereas Exchange stores folders on a different computer — known as a *server* — which is located someplace else on your office network. Exchange folders are meant to be shared with other people, while usually only one person uses a set of Outlook folders. If you use Outlook on a laptop and you need to use information from Exchange Server while you're traveling, you can create your own copy of the Exchange folder on your laptop. When you return from your trip with all your work finished, you can synchronize the copy of the folder on your laptop that you've used to make it match the copy that everyone shares on the company's server.

I could go on extolling the benefits you get from Microsoft Exchange Server, but most folks have no choice about whether the program is available to them. As I write this, only a small proportion of computer users also use Microsoft Exchange Server, but the computer business changes quickly, so, again, you have to wait and see.

Microsoft Office and Outlook

Outlook was originally introduced as part of the Microsoft Office suite. And, as you can guess, Outlook was designed to cooperate fully with other Office programs. Drag-and-drop techniques, cut and paste, and all sorts of other common tasks work throughout the suite. A few of the highlights follow.

Introducing Office Assistant

The little critter that pops up every time you press the F1 key is called the Office Assistant. You can leave the Assistant on-screen all the time if you want, or you can click the Close button at the upper-right corner of the Assistant window to make it go away.

When you ask for help, the Assistant opens a window in which you can type your question in plain English. In most cases, the Assistant makes sense of your question and then gives you a range of possible answers.

Office Assistant

If you leave the Office Assistant open all the time, the Assistant takes over most of the dialog boxes that you usually see when using Office applications. The result is that when you close an Outlook item, it's the Assistant that asks `Do you want to save changes?`.

Sometimes a small lightbulb appears in the upper-right corner of the Assistant's window. This lightbulb means that the Assistant has a tip in mind to help you do what it thinks you're trying to do. Fortunately, the Assistant remains quiet unless you click the bulb to get the hint.

Making Outlook talk to Word

Outlook was made to work well with Microsoft Word, so it's no surprise that you can use the two in tandem. Oddly, Microsoft left out a few details, so here are some things you need to do to get the most out of the two programs when you use them together.

If you want to have the power of Word at your disposal when creating e-mail, you have to tell Outlook that you want to use Word as your e-mail editor.

To use Word as your e-mail editor, follow these steps:

   1. Choose Tools⇨Options from the Outlook menu to open the Options dialog box.

2. Click the Mail Format tab in the Options dialog box and then choose Microsoft Word from the list box that says `Send in this message format`.

3. Click OK to close the Options dialog box.

After you choose Word as your e-mail editor, you can use the powerful formatting features of Word for all your e-mail messages. Things like bulleted lists and paragraph numbering, tables, graphics, and special text effects are available to you. These features wouldn't be available otherwise.

Remember, when you're using Word as your e-mail editor, many advanced formatting features that you can add to your e-mail can only be read by recipients who also use Microsoft Word and Outlook. In some cases, using Word as your e-mail editor also makes Outlook perform pretty slowly, so you may do just as well choosing plain text or HTML as your message format.

You can insert an address from your Outlook Contact list into a Word document by clicking a single button. Unfortunately, Microsoft didn't put that button on the Word toolbar, so you have to add it.

To add the Address Book button to the Word toolbar, follow these steps:

1. Open Microsoft Word and then choose Tools➪Customize to open the Customize dialog box.

2. Click the Commands tab to view the list available of commands.

3. Click Insert in the Categories box to reveal the list of Insert commands in the Commands list on the right side of the screen.

4. Scroll down to the words Address Book near the end of the Commands list box.

5. Drag the Address Book icon up to the Word toolbar. The Address Book icon joins the other icons on the toolbar.

Whew! Fortunately, you have to install the Address Book icon only once. After you install the Address Book, you can go right ahead and insert an address from your Outlook Contact list anywhere in any Word document in a jiffy.

To insert an address from your Outlook Contact list, follow these steps:

1. Open any document in Microsoft Word.

2. Click your mouse at the point in the document where you want to place an address. The insertion point (a vertical flashing bar) appears at the spot where you click.

3. Click the Address Book icon in the Word toolbar to open the Select Name dialog box.

4. After the Select Name dialog box opens, choose Contacts from the text box labeled Show Names to make the names from your Contact list appear.

5. From the list at the bottom of the Select Name dialog box, choose the name of the person whose address you want to enter.

6. Click OK to make the address of the person you picked appear in your document.

As you use the Address Book icon, you may notice the scroll-down button (triangle) just to the right of the icon. After you click the triangle, a list appears that contains the last 16 people whose addresses you entered by using the Address Book icon. To enter the address of one of the 16 people listed, just click his or her name; you don't have to go through the Select Name dialog box.

Making Outlook work with PowerPoint

If you're making a PowerPoint presentation at a meeting, you may need to make a note to do something as a result of the meeting. You can use the PowerPoint Meeting Minder feature to enter items in your Outlook Task list without leaving your PowerPoint presentation.

To enter items using the PowerPoint Meeting Minder feature, follow these steps:

1. In PowerPoint, choose Tools⇨Meeting Minder to open the Meeting Minder dialog box.

2. Click the Action Items tab.

3. Fill in the appropriate information in the Description, Assigned To, and Due Date boxes.

4. Click Add in order to make each item appear on the list of Action Items.

5. After your list is complete, click the Export button to open the Meeting Minder Export dialog box.

6. Click the check box that says Post Action Items to Microsoft Outlook.

7. Click Export Now to export action items to your Task list. The dialog boxes disappear, and you're returned to your PowerPoint presentation. Later, when you check your Task list, you see the action items that you exported listed there.

Options

You can customize Outlook to meet your needs. Adding, renaming, or deleting parts of the screen are easy to do, according to how you work. You can also make Outlook begin each session by showing you the information that you think is most important.

Add an icon to the Outlook Bar

After you get used to using Outlook, you may want to create more icons in the Outlook Bar. Because each icon in the Outlook Bar is a shortcut to a folder or resource on your computer, you can save some time by adding a few well-chosen icons.

The principle for adding icons is the same no matter what you're creating an icon to do.

Here's how to add an icon to the Outlook Bar:

1. Choose View⇨Folder List.

2. Right-click a folder for which you want to add an icon to the Outlook Bar. The shortcut menu appears.

3. Choose Add to Outlook Bar from the shortcut menu.

AutoArchive

You can save a lot of information in Outlook. After you store enough items, however, Outlook starts to slow down. To keep the program speedy, Outlook periodically sends older items to the archive file. The files are still available, but Outlook doesn't have to dredge them up every time you start the program.

You can set up Outlook to send items to the archives automatically after the items reach a certain age.

To set up automatic archiving, follow these steps:

1. Choose Tools➪Options to open the Options dialog box.

2. Click the Other tab.

3. Click the AutoArchive button to open the AutoArchive dialog box.

4. Click the check box that says AutoArchive every XX days and fill in the number of days you want between automatic archive sessions. If the box is already checked and you want AutoArchiving on, leave the box alone.

5. Click OK to close the AutoArchive dialog box.

6. Click OK again to close the Options dialog box.

After AutoArchiving is set up, when Outlook is ready to send items to the archive, you see a dialog box that asks whether or not you want the items sent to the archive.

If you choose not to use AutoArchiving, you can always archive items manually by choosing File➪Archive.

Outlook data files

All the items you create with Outlook and all the e-mail you send and receive are stored in one enormous file, called a *message store.* The file name of your message store ends with the letters PST. If you're trying to find your Outlook files so that you can back them up, use the Windows Find utility and search for files called *.PST. The largest file you find by that name is probably your Outlook data file.

Copying your MAILBOX.PST file to a floppy disk is not really an option. The file is usually 10 or 20 times too large to fit on a floppy disk.

Undo

Undo can be a lifesaver when you goof and need to fix your goof quickly. Just press Ctrl+Z. Outlook has only a one-level undo, which means that if you make two goofs in a row, you can only undo the last one. If you goof and then change modules by clicking an icon in the Outlook Bar, you can't go back and undo the mistake.

Specialized Applications

Outlook was designed with expansion in mind. Names, addresses, and files are important things to keep track of. Clever program-mers release new modules for Outlook every day. The Microsoft Web site on the Internet offers a collection of sample applications to expand the range of things you can do with Outlook. You can go to the Microsoft Web site right from Outlook.

Downloading specialized applications

You can get these sample applications free from the Microsoft site on the Internet. The sample applications include expense report applications, project management programs, and even cute little programs for keeping your recipes or making entries to your diary.

To pick up (or *download,* in tech talk) your free sample applica-tions, follow these steps:

1. Choose Help➪Microsoft on the Web➪Free Stuff to log on to the Microsoft site on the World Wide Web and see the list of free sample applications that are available for Outlook.

2. Click the name of a sample application that you want to use, such as Expense Reports, Project Management, Recipes, or Diary. If your browser is Microsoft Internet Explorer, a dialog box appears, asking if you want to open the file or save the file to disk.

3. Choose Save It to Disk.

The Save dialog box opens, showing you the name of the folder in which your file will be saved.

Note the name of the folder in the Save In box; that's where you install the new sample application after downloading the file. If you're not sure about which folder is the best place to save the file you're about to download, click the scroll-down menu (triangle) in the Save In box; then choose Desktop to make your new file go to the Windows 95 Desktop.

4. Click OK and wait for the File Transfer dialog box that shows up to disappear.

After a few minutes, the File Transfer dialog box disappears, which means that the file you need in order to install your new sample application is now on your computer. Now you're ready to install the sample application to make it work in Outlook.

A word of caution: Many of the sample applications that you find on the Microsoft Web site are useful only if you're using Outlook on a network that is also running Microsoft Exchange Server. Microsoft sometimes doesn't tell you which applications are useful for stand-alone (non-network) users, so, unfortunately, you're on your own. If you're on a network with Exchange Server, check with your network administrator before adding new applications.

After you download your brand-new sample application, you need to install it. Double-click the icon for the new file and follow the instructions that appear in the dialog boxes.

Each sample application is a little different, so you have to read the instructions carefully. I wish I could give you full instructions on all the sample applications, but Microsoft offers new sample applications every week, so I can't predict what you'll be dealing with.

Installing applications into Outlook

After you have downloaded and installed a new application, you would think that Outlook would be ready to use the new program right away, right? Not always. The programs that Microsoft offers on the Web site create a file on your computer that Outlook can use, but you have to take a few more steps to get Outlook actually to use the new program. I hope that Microsoft improves its installation procedures by the time you read this, but there's no guarantee, so I guide you through a few of the details here. You have to install an application only once, so don't despair if this next bit seems a little too geeky; you never have to go through this again.

If you're not comfortable with technical stuff such as installing programs, you may want to get help when you're installing these programs. If your local computer guru isn't familiar with Outlook, show him or her this section of the chapter. I include this section because I find that the Microsoft installation instructions are pretty flaky and often incorrect; even a computer guru would need ESP to get this stuff to work right the first time.

To add a sample application to Outlook, here's what you do:

1. Choose File⇨Open⇨Other Outlook File to open the Open Personal Folders dialog box.

2. Double-click the icon for the file whose name corresponds to the application you downloaded; the Expense Report program is called Expense Report.pst, the Recipe program is called Recipes.pst, and so on.

3. Choose View⇨Folder List to open the Folder List. The Folder List includes a folder with a name that corresponds to your new application, such as Expense Reports for Expense reports and Recipes for the Recipe program. The new folder has an icon with a plus just to its left.

4. Click the plus sign to the left of the folder for the new application you want to install. Two subfolders appear, one with the name of your new application.

5. Right-click the name of the subfolder with the name of your new application to open the shortcut menu.

6. Choose Add to Outlook Bar from the shortcut menu to make an icon for your new application appear in the Outlook Bar.

7. Choose View⇨Folder List again to make the Folder List disappear.

There! Whew! Aren't you glad you have to do that only once? (Only once for each sample application, that is.) Microsoft isn't the only outfit creating extra applications for Outlook, but their programs are the most readily available — and they're free.

Outlook Express and Other Flavors of Outlook

The folks at Microsoft were mighty proud after they released Outlook — so proud, in fact, that they gave the name Outlook to a second, totally different product a few weeks later. *Outlook Express* is a program that used to be called Internet Mail and News before going big-time and getting a new name. I'm sure that Microsofties find the new names perfectly sensible, but I become very confused when I have to deal with two different products that go by the same name.

Like regular Outlook, Outlook Express can exchange e-mail. But Outlook Express can't do many of the fancy tricks with your mail that you can do with regular Outlook. For example, you can't drag an e-mail message to the Contacts folder to create a new Contact record or flag messages to remind you to take action.

However, Outlook Express can do tricks that regular Outlook hasn't learned yet, such as reading Internet newsgroups. (*Newsgroups* are places on the Internet where people can read each other's messages and post replies to any message.) See also the discussion on Public Folders in the section "Microsoft Exchange Server" earlier in this part. The Public Folders are very similar to newsgroups, except that newsgroups are available to anyone on the Internet. Public Folders can be used only by people you work with.

If you have Outlook 98, you also have Outlook Express. You can start Outlook Express by choosing Go⇨News from the Outlook menu bar. After you start Outlook Express from within Outlook, you see a special version of Outlook Express that only enables you to read and contribute to Internet newsgroups.

Microsoft has hinted strongly that someday regular Outlook (which you have to pay for) will be able to read Internet newsgroups, just as you can with Outlook Express (which is free). Don't worry if this situation confuses you: It confuses everybody. For more about Outlook Express, see my full-sized version of this book, *Microsoft Outlook 98 For Windows For Dummies* published by IDG Books Worldwide, Inc.

Outlook Today

Outlook is designed to pull all your personal information into one handy package. The Outlook Today page pulls all the Outlook data that you're likely to need to see at any moment onto a single screen. All you need to do is click the Outlook Today icon in the Outlook Bar. If you can't see the Outlook Today icon, choose Go⇨Outlook Today from the menu bar.

The Outlook Today page is similar to a page on the World Wide Web. Most of the text on the page is made of something called *Hypertext,* which means that if you click the text, the screen changes to show you the full text of the Outlook module or item that it refers to. For example, if you click the word Mail in the Outlook Today page, the screen switches to a view of your Inbox and displays all the messages that are waiting for you.

I like to print Outlook Today to help remind me of what I need to do each day. That's the best way I know of to see a single summary of my most current appointments, tasks, and messages. If you want to print your Outlook Today page, click the Outlook Today icon in the Outlook Bar and then choose File⇨Print from the menu bar.

E-Mail

The e-mail Inbox is the first thing you see when you start Outlook, and if e-mail is the only thing you ever use Outlook for, you still get your money's worth.

You can exchange e-mail with television personalities, the White House, and yes, even Microsoft (though you may have trouble getting Microsoft to answer).

When you use Outlook to create and receive your e-mail, you have lots of options for viewing, sorting, and organizing your messages that can make your messages more useful. You can assign a category to each message, and then group the messages you've sent by category to review what you've done.

In this part . . .

- ✓ Creating e-mail messages
- ✓ Answering your e-mail
- ✓ Sending and receiving e-mail online
- ✓ Using views
- ✓ Printing your messages

About the Inbox Screen

The main Inbox screen enables you to view a list of your e-mail and helps you manage the messages you send and receive. You can create folders for storing each message according to what the message is about, who sent it to you, or when you got it.

Menu Bar   Toolbar

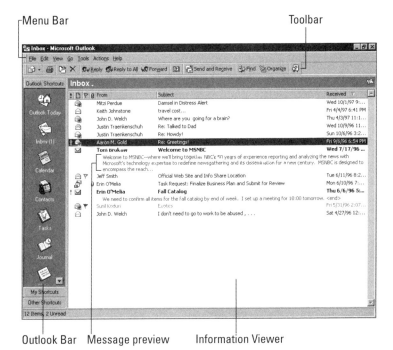

Outlook Bar   Message preview   Information Viewer

You can change the arrangement of what you see in the Inbox by changing the view. (A *view* is a method of organizing the information you see in Outlook.) Each view has a name, such as Message, AutoPreview, By Conversation Topic, and so on.

To change from one view to another, simply choose View↩ Current View and pick the view you want from the list that appears.

Accessing your Inbox

Your Inbox contains your list of incoming e-mail. Even if you've never exchanged e-mail with anybody, or even if you don't *know* anybody, you see at least one message in your Inbox the first time you start Outlook — the "Welcome to Microsoft Outlook" message. Isn't that nice of Microsoft?

To open and read an e-mail message, follow these steps:

1. Switch to the Inbox by clicking the Inbox icon on the Outlook Bar.

2. Double-click the title of the message that you want to read. The message opens, using the whole screen so that you can read your message.

3. Press Esc to close the message screen.

If you want to read the message that follows on your list, press Ctrl+>.

Opening the Message form

Whenever you want to read or write a message, open the Message form by double-clicking the title of the message in the Inbox (or whatever folder you filed the message in). When you double-click the title of a message, the Message form screen appears. The Message form has many of the same tools and menus as the main Outlook screen but includes a large message box at the bottom that contains either the message you're reading or space for the message you're about to write.

Send button   Text box

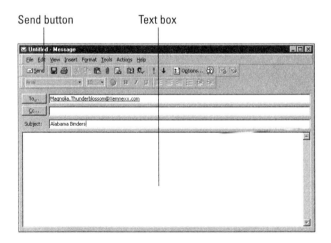

The little figures on the Message form toolbar do things that are specific to writing and reading e-mail messages, such as reply, print, or mark as high or low priority, and the up and down arrows enable you to read the next message on your Inbox list.

Creating and Sending Messages

If you know an e-mail address, you can send a message. You don't even need to have anything to say, although it's usually a good idea to have a thought or two worth sending so that people find your e-mail worth reading. To create a message:

1. Switch to the Inbox by clicking the Inbox icon on the Outlook Bar to show your list of messages.

2. Click the New Mail Message button (or press Ctrl+N) to open the New Message form.

3. Click the To text box and enter the e-mail address of the person to whom you're sending the message.

For people whose e-mail addresses you've included in your Contact list, just enter the person's name. If Outlook knows the e-mail address of the person whose name you enter, a solid black underline appears under the name.

Another approach is to click the To button to open the Select Name dialog box. Then double-click the name of the person to whom you're sending the message from the list on the left side of the box; click OK to return to your Message form.

4. Click the Cc text box and enter the e-mail address of the people to whom you want to send a copy of your message.

5. Enter the subject of the message in the Subject box.

6. Enter the text of your message in the text box.

7. Click the Send button (or press Alt+S) to close the Message form and send your message on its way.

If you send your e-mail over an online service, you also have to press F5 to deliver your message from the Outbox to your online service. If you're on an office network that uses Microsoft Exchange Server, your message goes directly to the recipient when you click Send.

Attaching files to your messages

When you want to send someone a document, a picture, or a spreadsheet that you don't want to include in the message itself, you can add it to the message as an attachment. You don't even have to send an actual message; just save the file you're working on and send it along as an attachment. Here's how:

1. Switch to the Inbox by clicking the Inbox icon on the Outlook Bar.

2. Choose File⇨New⇨Mail Message (or press Ctrl+N) to open the New Message form.

 3. Click the paper-clip button in the Message form toolbar. The list of files appears.

4. Click the name of the file that you want to send. The filename is highlighted to show that you've selected it.

5. Click OK. The list of files disappears, and an icon representing your file appears in the text box of the Message form.

6. Enter your message if you have a message to send. You don't have to send a message if you don't have anything to say.

7. Click the To button to open the Select Name dialog box.

8. Select a name from your address book.

9. Click the To button to move the name you selected to the Message Recipients box on the right side of the dialog box.

10. Click OK to close the Select Name dialog box and return to the Message form.

11. Click the Subject text box and enter a subject for your message.

12. Click the Send button to close the Message form.

If you want to e-mail a document while you're creating it in a
Microsoft Office application, you can eliminate most of this
procedure by choosing File➪Send To➪Mail Recipient and then
following Steps 7 through 12.

Indicating message importance

Some messages are very important to both you and the person
getting the message. Other messages aren't so important, but you
send them as a matter of routine to keep people informed. Outlook
enables you to designate the importance of a message to help your
recipients make good use of their time. When you open the
Message form to create a message, two icons on the Message form
toolbar enable you to select the importance of your message:

+ To assign High importance, click the Importance: High button
  on the Message form toolbar.

+ To assign Low importance, click the Importance: Low button
  on the Message form toolbar.

An icon corresponding to the importance of the message appears
in the first column of the Message List.

Formatting message text

You can spice up your messages with text formatting, such as
boldface, italics, or different typefaces, whether you use Outlook
alone or with Microsoft Office. You can also tell Outlook to use
Microsoft Word 97 as your e-mail editor, which means that each
time you open an e-mail message, Microsoft Word steps in and
automatically adjusts the appearance of the message. When you
create a new message with Word as your e-mail editor, you have
the power to add fancy-looking elements to your message, such as
tables, special text effects (like flashing text), and you can use all
the other powerful features of Word.

The shortcoming to using Word as your e-mail editor is that you
have to wait several seconds for Word to launch and format each
message before you read it. If you're too impatient to wait a few
seconds for each message to be formatted (I'll admit it: I am), you
can get away without using Word as your e-mail editor.

To format text in a message without using Microsoft Word as your
e-mail editor, use the tools on the Formatting toolbar in the
Message form.

If you've ever used a word processor in Windows, the steps you take to format text in an Outlook message will be familiar to you: Just click the button for the type of formatting you want to add to your text, and then type your text.

+ To format text you've already typed, hold down your mouse button and drag the mouse over the text to select it. Then click the button for the type of formatting you want to give to your text, such as bold, italic, and so on.

+ To set the typeface of your text, click the scroll-down button at the end of the font menu and choose the name of the font you want to use.

+ To set the size of your text, click the scroll-down button on the font size menu and highlight the font size you want.

+ To set the color of your text, click the color button and choose a color. There are only a few colors you can choose, but your choices include teal, fuchsia, and aqua, so there's certainly something to match any décor.

+ To make your text bold, italic, or underlined, click the Bold, Italic, or Underline button (or press Ctrl+B, Ctrl+I, or Ctrl+U, respectively).

+ To align your text to the left, center, or right, click the Align Left, Center, or Align Right button. (I bet you're starting to see a pattern here.)

✦ To create a bulleted list, click the bullets button. (This is not the button to click when you want to shoot your computer.)

✦ To indent your text, click the Increase Indent button. To reduce the amount you've indented your text, click the Decrease Indent button.

Remember, when you send e-mail to people who don't use Outlook, the formatting you apply in Outlook will often be lost. You may enjoy seeing all your messages when you type them in bold fuchsia, but many of your readers won't get the same pleasure when they read your messages.

Marking messages as Personal, Private, or Confidential

You can designate any message you create as either Personal, Private, or Confidential. How you designate the message makes very little difference to Outlook. Personal and Confidential messages are no different from any other message.

Private messages differ slightly from other messages in that, when you reply to or forward a Private message, other Outlook users can't change the text of the message you send.

Here's how to make your message Personal, Private, or Confidential while you're creating the message:

1. Click the Options button on the message toolbar to view the Options dialog box.

2. Click the scroll-down button at the right end of the Sensitivity box to see the choices available.

3. Choose Normal, Personal, Private, or Confidential.

4. Choose File⇨Close (or press Alt+F4) to close the message screen.

Messages marked Personal, Private, or Confidential can still be read by people other than your intended recipient, especially messages on a corporate LAN.

Saving copies of your message

Outlook normally saves all sent messages in your Sent Items folder, but you can turn off this option. If you've turned this feature off, here's how to turn it back on:

1. Choose Tools⇨Options to open the Options dialog box.

2. Click the E-mail Options button.

3. Click the Save Copies of Messages in Sent Items Folder option so that a mark appears in the check box.

4. Click OK to close the Options dialog box.

I find it extremely handy to have copies of my sent messages available. I use them for record keeping, checking my work, and sometimes just to be sure that a message went out.

Spell checking

Heaven knows you want to spell everything correctly when you send out an e-mail message. Who knows how many people will see the message, or if a million years from now someone will discover your old messages on an archeological dig? Fortunately, you can spell check all your messages before sending them out.

1. Choose Tools⇨Spelling (or press F7) to start the spelling checker. If everything is perfect, a dialog box opens, saying `The spelling check is complete.` If so, you can click OK and get on with your life.

2. In the highly unlikely event that you've misspelled something, the Spelling dialog box opens and shows you the error (it's probably the computer's fault) along with a list of suggested (that is, correct) spellings.

3. If one of the suggested spellings is the one you really meant, click the spelling you want. If none of the suggested spellings is quite what you have in mind, enter the spelling you want in the Change To box.

4. Click the Change button.

5. Should there be any other errors (heaven *forfend!*), repeat Steps 3 and 4 until you've eradicated all misspellings.

The spelling checker often thinks that technical terms like *WYSIWYG* and proper names like *Englebert Humperdinck* are misspellings (well, maybe they are), but you can increase your spelling checker's vocabulary by clicking the <u>A</u>dd button when the spelling checker zeros in on words like that. You can also click <u>I</u>gnore if the spelling checker stops on a weird word that you encounter infrequently.

If you've chosen to use Microsoft Word as your e-mail editor (**see also** the section in Part I called "Making Outlook talk to Word"), a wavy red underline appears beneath misspelled words as soon as you enter them. When you see a wavy red underline beneath a word, just correct the spelling right then and there so that you don't have to use the spelling checker. When you right-click a misspelled word, a shortcut menu appears with the correct spelling; click the correct spelling and you can go right on entering text.

Using stationery

Stationery is designed to make your messages convey a visual impression about you. You can make your message look uniquely important, businesslike, or just plain fun with the right choice of stationery.

1. Choose Actio<u>n</u>s⇨New <u>M</u>ail Message Using⇨Stationery. The Select a Stationery dialog box appears, containing a list of each type of stationery you can choose.

2. Double-click the type of stationery that you want to use.

3. Fill in your message.

4. Click the To button to open the Select Name dialog box.

5. Double-click the name of the person to whom you want to send the message. This action copies the name to the Message Recipients list.

6. Click OK to close the Select Name dialog box.

7. Click Send to close the Message form and send your message along.

If the command called New Mail Message Using on the Actions menu isn't black and doesn't work when you click it, you need to turn the feature on. Choose Tools⇨Options, click the Mail Format tab, and then choose HTML from the scroll-down menu at the top of the Mail Format page.

Handling Incoming Messages

You can reply to messages while you read them or you can wait until later.

Sending a reply

To reply to a message, follow these steps:

1. Switch to the Inbox by clicking the Inbox icon on the Outlook Bar.

2. Double-click the title of the message to which you want to reply. Doing so shows the text of the message to which you're replying. You don't absolutely have to open a message to send a reply; you can click the name of a message once to select the message to reply to and then click the Reply button.

 3. If you want to reply only to the people who are named in the From line, click the Reply button (or press Alt+R) to open the New Message form.

 4. If you want to reply to the people who are named in the Cc line as well as the people named on the From line, click the Reply to All button (or press Alt+L) to open the New Message form.

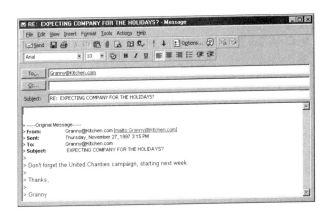

5. Enter your reply in the message box.

6. Click the Send button (or press Alt+S) to close the New Message form and send your message on its way.

The text of the message to which you're replying is automatically included in your reply unless you turn that option off by choosing Tools⇨Options and then choosing your options under the Reading tab.

Deleting a message

If you get mail from the Internet, you can expect lots of junk mail. You may also get lots of e-mail at work. I understand that Bill Gates gets scads of e-mail. Maybe that's why deleting messages in Outlook is so easy. Just follow these steps:

1. Switch to the Inbox by clicking the Inbox icon on the Outlook Bar.

2. Click the title of the message that you want to delete.

 3. Click the Delete tool on the toolbar or press the Delete key to make your message disappear.

If you accidentally delete something you meant to save, choose Edit⇨Undo (or press Ctrl+Z) right away, and your message reappears.

Flagging your e-mail messages as a reminder

Some people use their incoming e-mail messages as an informal task list. Flagging is designed to make it easier to use your Inbox as a Task list by adding individual reminders to each message you get (or even to messages you send).

1. Switch to the Inbox by clicking the Inbox icon on the
Outlook Bar.

2. Double-click the message that you want to flag, and the
message reopens.

3. Choose Actions⇨Flag for Follow Up (or press Ctrl+Shift+G) to
open the Flag for Follow Up dialog box.

4. Click the Flag To text box and enter your reminder, such as
Call headquarters. You can also click the scroll-down button
at the end of the Flag To text box and choose a reminder, such
as Follow Up.

5. Click the Reminder box and type the date on which you want
the reminder flag to appear. Remember, you can enter dates in
plain English by entering something like **Next Wednesday** or
in three weeks, and let Outlook figure out the actual date.

6. Click OK.

A little red flag appears next to your message in the Inbox. Another
clever way you can take advantage of flagging is to attach a flag to
a message when you're sending it to someone else. If you flag a
message you're sending to someone else, a reminder pops up on
his or her computer at the time you designated. I'd bet Bill Gates
sends out lots of flagged messages, wouldn't you?

My how time flies! If you've put a flag on a message that's due to
appear before you're ready to do what the flag calls for, here's how
you can change the due date:

1. Switch to the Inbox by clicking the Inbox icon on the
Outlook Bar.

2. Double-click the message to open the Message form.

3. Choose Actions⇨Flag for Follow Up (or press Ctrl+Shift+G) to
open the Flag for Follow Up dialog box.

4. Click the Reminder box and type the new date for when you
want the reminder flag to appear.

5. Click OK to close the Flag for Follow Up dialog box.

6. Press Esc to close the Message form.

Your message is still flagged as it was before, but the reminder pops up at a different time or gives a different message.

Forwarding a message

If you get a message that you want to pass on to someone else, just forward it:

1. Switch to the Inbox by clicking the Inbox icon on the Outlook Bar.

2. Click the title of the message that you want to forward. This action highlights the message.

3. Click the Forward button from the Outlook toolbar (or press Alt+W) to open the New Message form.

4. Click the To text box and enter the e-mail address of the person to whom you're forwarding the message.

5. Click the Cc text box and enter the e-mail addresses of the people to whom you want to forward a copy of your message.

6. In the text box, enter any comments that you want to add to the message.

7. Click the Send button (or press Alt+S) to close the Message form and send your message on its way.

You can also forward a message as you read it by clicking the Forward button on the Message form toolbar, which is visible when you open a message to read it.

Marking messages as Read or Unread

Outlook notices which messages you've read and which messages you haven't read. AutoPreview shows you only the first few lines of messages you haven't read, and the Unread Messages view hides messages completely after you've read them.

You may want to mark a message as Unread even though you've read it; for example, if you don't have time to deal with the message the first time you see it, you may want to be reminded to read it again. You also may mark a message as Read if you see all you need to know in the three-line AutoPreview.

Here's how you mark a message as read if you haven't read it and don't plan to:

1. Switch to the Inbox by clicking the Inbox icon on the Outlook Bar.

2. Click the title of the message that you want to mark as read. This action highlights the message.

3. Choose Edit⇨Mark as Read (or press Ctrl+Q).

To mark a message as Unread, follow the same steps, but choose Edit⇨Mark as Unread.

Previewing messages

You can usually get the gist of an incoming e-mail message in the first few lines, so Outlook shows you the first few lines of all unread messages, if you want. The AutoPreview feature is turned on the first time you use Outlook, but you can also turn it off if you want.

To turn AutoPreview on, follow these steps:

1. Switch to the Inbox by clicking the Inbox icon on the Outlook Bar.

2. Choose View⇨AutoPreview.

AutoPreview shows you the first few lines of the messages you haven't read yet. You can mark messages as Read or Unread in order to keep the AutoPreview pane open as you want.

AutoPreview may be the only way you'll ever want to view your Inbox. If you get a lot of messages, previewing your messages saves time. You can also take advantage of the Preview Pane to view the contents of each message in the lower half of the Information Viewer while your list of messages appears in the upper half. To turn the Preview Pane on (or off) choose View⇨Preview Pane.

Saving a message as a file

You may need to save the contents of a message you receive so that you can use the text in another program. For example, you may want to use a desktop publishing program to add the text to your monthly newsletter or even to your page on the Internet.

To save a message as a file, follow these steps:

1. Choose File⇨Save As (or press F12) to open the Save As dialog box.

2. Click the scroll-down button at the end of the Save In box to choose the drive to which you want to save the file.

3. Double-click the name of the folder in which you want to save the file to reveal the list of files in the folder.

4. Click the File Name text box and type the name that you want to give the file.

5. If you want to change the type of the file, click the scroll-down button at the end of the Save as Type box and then choose a file type.

6. Click Save (or press Enter) to close the Save As dialog box.

Your message is saved as a text file in the folder you clicked. You can open the text file with any word-processing program.

Setting options for replies

You can use the Options dialog box to control the way messages look when you send replies. If you're not fussy about things like that, you can leave this option alone and let Outlook take care of the formatting for you.

1. Choose Tools➪Options to open the Options dialog box.

2. Click the E-mail Options button to show the choices available for message replies and forwarded messages.

3. Click the triangle at the right end of the When Replying to a Message box to reveal the list of styles that are available to you for replies.

4. Choose the style that you prefer to use for replies. As you choose different styles, the little diagram on the right side of the box changes to show what your choice looks like.

5. Click the scroll-down button at the right end of the When Forwarding a Message box. Another diagram to the right of the menu shows what your choice looks like.

6. Choose the style that you prefer to use for forwarding messages.

7. Click OK to close the Options dialog box.

If you're using Microsoft Word as your e-mail editor, you can also take advantage of the powerful features for formatting text that come with Word, including tables, bullets and numbering, and Autoformatting. For more about what you can do with Microsoft Word, see *Word 97 For Windows For Dummies* by Dan Gookin (IDG Books Worldwide, Inc.).

Tagging replies with your name

When you reply to an e-mail message, Outlook includes the text of the original message in your reply. Including the original text helps the person you're replying to remember what you're talking about. When you mix what you've written with what the other person wrote in the first place, however, the message can get confusing. Outlook gives you the option of automatically inserting your name before everything you add to a reply. Here's how you can turn this option on (or off):

1. Choose Tools⇨Options to open the Options dialog box.

2. Click the E-mail Options button to show the choices available for message replies and forwarded messages.

3. Click the Mark My Comments With check box. A check mark appears in the box.

4. In the Mark My Comments With text box, enter the text that you want to accompany your annotations.

5. Click OK.

If you use Microsoft Word as your e-mail editor, the tagging option is not available because it's unnecessary. Microsoft Word formats your reply more neatly than Outlook alone, so the reply is easier to understand.

Using the Rules Wizard

The Rules Wizard reads your incoming and outgoing e-mail and takes an action of your choice. You can make Outlook display a pop-up announcement when important messages arrive, or make a rude noise when you get messages from certain people, or it can just file certain types of messages in certain folders.

Wizards are little tools that Microsoft adds to all Office programs to guide you through multistep processes and help you make the choices you need to make. The Rules Wizard asks you questions at each step of the process of creating a rule to help you create the rule you want.

You can create literally thousands of different kinds of rules with the Rules Wizard. As you explore the Rules Wizard, you'll discover many types of rules that you'll find useful. I describe only one rule here, which I think most people find useful; this one moves a message that arrives from a certain person to a certain folder.

1. If you're not in the Inbox, click the Inbox icon on the Outlook Bar.

2. Choose Tools⇔Rules Wizard to open the Rules Wizard dialog box.

3. Click the <u>N</u>ew button to open a dialog box for creating new rules.

4. Choose the type of rule you want to create by clicking the box cleverly named Which Type of Rule Do You Want to Create? The Rules Wizard offers several common types of rules that you might want to create, such as Move Messages from Someone, Assign Categories to Sent Messages, or Notify Me When Important Messages Come. Another choice is Build as I Go, which is the option to use when you want to create rules that don't quite fit the Rules Wizard's predefined types. For this example, I suggest choosing Move New Messages from Someone. The words `Apply this rule after the message arrives from people or distribution list move it to the specified folder` appear in the <u>R</u>ule Description box at the bottom of the dialog box.

5. Click the first piece of underlined text in the <u>R</u>ule Description box, which is `people or distribution list.` Your address book opens to enable you to choose the name of a person to put into your rule.

6. Choose the name of the person whose messages you want to move to a new folder; in this case, you want to move your boss's name from your address book. When you do, your boss's name replaces the words `people or distribution list`.

7. Click the next piece of underlined text in the Rule Description box — the word `specified`. Another dialog box opens to enable you to choose the folder to which you want to move the message.

8. Click the name of the folder to which you want to move messages. The name of the folder you choose appears in the sentence in the Rule Description box.

9. Click Finish to complete your rule. The first Rules Wizard dialog box appears with a list of all your rules. Each rule has a check box next to it. You can turn rules on and off by clicking the check boxes; if there's a check mark next to a rule, it's turned on, otherwise the rule is turned off.

10. Click OK to close the Rules Wizard.

You don't have to limit yourself to making rules for incoming mail. You also can tell the Rules Wizard to act on the messages you send out, such as attaching flags or assigning categories to messages that go to the people you designate or to messages that have certain words in the subject line.

Managing Folders

You can leave all your incoming e-mail messages in your Inbox if you like, but filing your messages in another folder makes more sense, because you can see at a glance which messages you've already dealt with and classified, and which ones have just arrived in your Inbox. I like to move messages out of my Inbox as soon as I've read them or taken appropriate action. For example, in the course of writing this book, I receive dozens of messages about Outlook and the book. I save all the messages about this book in a specific folder so that I don't have to waste time sorting through hundreds of old messages about other subjects when I need to find a message related to the book. I also like to keep the Inbox empty as often as possible; that way I know that if I see something sitting in my Inbox, it's new.

Creating a folder

Before you can file messages in a new folder, you need to create the folder. Here's how:

1. Click the Inbox icon to switch to your Inbox (if you're not already there).

2. Choose File⇨New⇨Folder (or press Ctrl+Shift+E) to open the Create New Folder dialog box.

3. Click the word Inbox in the list of folders at the bottom of the Create New Folder dialog box to highlight it.

4. In the <u>N</u>ame text box, type a name for your new folder.

5. Click OK to close the Create New Folder dialog box.

You can create as many folders as you like, but you can find things more easily if you minimize the number of folders you have to search.

Moving messages to another folder

After you've created extra folders for sorting and saving your incoming messages, you can move new messages to the different folders when they arrive.

To move messages to another folder:

1. Switch to the Inbox by clicking the Inbox icon on the Outlook Bar.

2. Click the title of the message that you want to move to highlight the message title.

3. Drag the message to the icon on the Outlook Bar for the folder in which you want to store it. The name of the file disappears from the list in the Inbox.

The folder to which you want to move the message isn't always visible in the Outlook Bar. If the folder to which you want to move your message isn't visible in the Outlook Bar, choose <u>E</u>dit⟶<u>M</u>ove to Folder to make a more complete list of folders appear (*see also* "The Folder List" in Part I). Then you can click the folder in which you want to file your message and press Enter.

 After you've made a habit of moving messages between folders, you can speed up the process by clicking the Move to Folder button. When you click the Move to Folder button, you see a list of the last 10 folders to which you've moved items. Click the name of a folder on the list, and your message is zapped directly to the folder of your choice.

Using the Sent Items folder

Outlook stores a copy of every message you send in the Sent Items folder unless you tell it to do otherwise. You can review and reread the messages you've sent by looking in the Sent Items folder. To get there, click the My Shortcuts divider in the Outlook Bar and then click the Sent Items icon. The same collection of views is available in the Sent Items folder as is available in the Inbox or any other mail folder (*see also* "Using and Choosing E-Mail Views" later in this part).

Sending and Receiving Online Mail

If you use Outlook to send mail to online services such as The Microsoft Network, CompuServe, or through an Internet service provider that you reach by telephone, your outgoing messages are stored in the Outbox until you choose Tools➪Send and Receive➪ All Accounts (or press F5). Your messages are then dispatched to your online service and sent on to your recipient.

Accessing the Outbox

To view or edit a message that's still stored in your Outbox, here's what you do:

1. Press Ctrl+Shift+O to see the list of messages in your Outbox.

2. Double-click the title of the message in the Outbox that you want to view or edit to open the message for editing.

3. Read the message and make any changes you want.

4. Click the Send button (or press Alt+S) to close the Message form and return to a view of your Outbox.

The titles of messages that are ready to be sent appear in italic text. If you see a message in the Outbox whose title is not italicized, that message won't be sent until you open the message (by double-clicking it) and then click the Send button (or press Alt+S). Messages in the Outbox stay there until you choose Tools➪Send and Receive (or press F5).

Checking for new mail

If you use an online service like CompuServe or The Microsoft Network for your e-mail, you need to tell Outlook to pick up the phone and log on to the service. When you do that, Outlook sends the messages you've created and collects the messages sent to you.

To check for new messages, follow these steps:

1. Choose Tools➪Send and Receive➪All Accounts (or press F5).

2. The Delivering Messages dialog box appears and remains on the screen until Outlook has checked messages on all your services.

In order to exchange messages with online services, you need to set up Outlook to use each service. *See also* the "Setting up online services" section later in this part.

Press F5 to check for new messages on any and all online services you've set up to communicate with Outlook.

Creating Personal Distribution Lists and Groups

When you send e-mail to the same group of people over and over, you can save lots of time by creating a list that contains the addresses of all the people in the group. Then when you send your message, rather than entering the name of each person on your list, you need only enter the name of the list.

Outlook 98 comes in two different versions, the Corporate version and the Internet Mail Only version. You can tell which one you have by checking the Tools menu. If you have a command called Tools➪Services, you have the Corporate version and you can create Personal Distribution Lists.

The Internet Mail Only version of Outlook 98 doesn't have a Tools➪Services command and it also doesn't have Personal Distribution Lists. However, it does enable you to create something called Groups, which are very similar to Personal Distribution Lists. You can tell that you have the Internet Mail Only version of Outlook 98 if you have a command named Tools➪Accounts. I wish Microsoft had created a less confusing arrangement for all of this, but that's how it is.

Here's how to create a Personal Distribution List:

1. Choose Tools➪Address Book to open the Address Book dialog box.

2. Choose File➪New Entry to open the New Entry dialog box.

3. Scroll to the bottom of the Entry Type box and click Personal Distribution List. Make sure that the space at the bottom of the dialog box that says `Put this entry in the` contains the words `Personal Address Book`.

4. Click OK to open the New Personal Distribution List Properties dialog box.

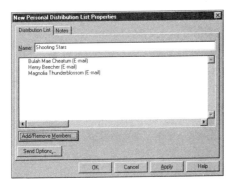

5. Enter a name for your new Personal Distribution List in the Name box.

6. Click Add/Remove Members to open the Edit Members dialog box.

7. Double-click the name of each person you want to include in your Personal Distribution List. As you double-click each name, the names you choose are copied into the Personal Distribution List box on the right side of the Edit Members dialog box.

8. Click OK after you've finished adding all the names you want to include in your Personal Distribution List.

If you have the Internet Mail Only version of Outlook 98, here's how you create groups:

1. Choose Tools⇨Address Book to open the Address Book dialog box.

2. Click the New Group button to open the Group properties dialog box.

3. Enter a name for your new group in the Group Name box.

4. Click the Select Members button to open the Select Group Members dialog box.

5. Double-click the name of each person you want to include in your group. As you double-click each name, the names you choose are copied into the Members box on the right side of the Select Group Members dialog box.

6. Click OK when you've finished adding all the names you want to include in your group.

When you want to send a message to everyone in one of your Groups or on your Personal Distribution Lists, just type the name you gave to the list in Step 3 in the To box of your message. You can have as many Groups or Personal Distribution Lists as you like. You can also make a group or list a member of another group or list. For example, you can have a list named Vice Presidents for all the VPs in your company, and also a list of Senior Management. If you make the Vice Presidents list a member of the Senior Management list, you only have to add new Vice Presidents to the Vice Presidents list; they'll automatically become a part of the Senior Management list as well.

Marking Remote Mail

If you get lots of mail, chances are that some of what you get is important and some isn't so important. When you're at your desk at home or the office, weeding out the unimportant messages is not such a problem. But if you need to keep up with important e-mail on your laptop while you're traveling, you may not have time to wade through the unimportant stuff.

Remote Mail dials your online service and shows you the names of the messages that are waiting for you. You can mark the messages that you think are important and have Outlook just get the messages you marked. Time is money, especially when you're checking your e-mail by long-distance telephone connections.

Here's how to use Remote Mail to pick and choose your messages.

1. Click the Inbox icon in the Outlook Bar to switch to the Inbox (if you're not already there).

2. Choose Tools➪Remote Mail➪Connect to open the Remote Mail dialog box.

3. Click the name of the online service on which you want to see the titles of your waiting messages.

A check mark appears next to the names of the services you select.

4. Click Next to open the Remote Connection Wizard dialog box.

5. Click the button that says Do Only the Following. A line for each message service you choose appears in the box that says something like Retrieve New Message Headers Via The Microsoft Network. Be sure that a check mark appears next to each service that you want to check.

6. Click Finish to start the Remote Mail session. The Remote Mail status box remains on the screen until the session is complete.

7. When the Remote Mail session is complete, the titles of any messages you have waiting on your online service appear in your Inbox with a special icon, indicating that the message is still at the online service, waiting for you to retrieve it. You can't read messages until you retrieve them. A new toolbar, called Remote, also appears.

 8. Click each message that you want to retrieve and then click the Mark to Retrieve button in the Remote toolbar. A second icon appears next to each message that you mark to retrieve.

 9. Click the Connect icon to open the Remote Connection Wizard dialog box again.

10. Check to see that a check mark is next to the name of the service from which you want to retrieve messages. Normally, the last service you used is still checked.

11. Click Next to move to the next step of the Remote Connection Wizard.

12. Click Finish to start the Remote Mail session. The Remote Mail status box remains on the screen until your messages are all retrieved.

13. Your messages appear in the Inbox. Double-click the names of the messages you want to read.

As you can see, the Remote Mail Wizard is pretty time consuming for something that's supposed to save you time. If you get really large amounts of e-mail, you'll find Remote Mail necessary from time to time. Normally, however, you're better off just choosing Tools⇨Send and Receive (or pressing F5).

Reading attachments

When you receive a message with a file attached (*see also* "Attaching files to your messages" earlier in this part), you need to open the attachment before you can read whatever is in the attachment. No problemo.

1. Double-click the name of the message that has an attachment you want to read. The Message form opens.

2. An icon in the body of the message represents each file attached to the message. Just double-click the icon to open the attachment; double-clicking the icon also launches the program that created the message.

An even faster way to get a peek at the contents of a file attached to a message you receive is to right-click the icon for the attachment and choose QuickView from the shortcut menu. You can't make changes to a document when you're using QuickView, but you can get a glimpse of what the attachment is about.

Setting up online services

Before you can use Outlook to exchange e-mail through an online service, such as CompuServe, America Online (AOL), or The Microsoft Network, or through an Internet service provider such as Netcom or the AT&T WorldNet Service, you have to set up Outlook to work with that particular service.

If you work in a large organization that uses Microsoft Exchange Server for its e-mail system, your system administrators will set up the Outlook 98 Corporate version for you. They probably don't want you setting up online services on the copy of Outlook 98 on your Desktop, so I won't get into it. You can still send e-mail to people on online services like CompuServe or AOL by typing their address in the To box of your message.

If you're using Outlook 98 somewhere other than on a large corporate network, you'll want to use the Outlook 98 Internet Mail Only version. The Internet Mail Only version enables you to set up e-mail accounts to work with most online services and Internet service providers. Although the method you use to set up any service is pretty similar, the exact details differ, and those differences are important. Before beginning to set up Outlook e-mail accounts, it's a good idea to check with the tech support people from your online service so that you understand the details. After you get the skinny from your online service, follow these steps to set up e-mail accounts on the Outlook 98 Internet Mail Only version:

1. Choose Tools➪Accounts.

2. Click the Add button and then choose Mail from the shortcut menu to start the Internet Connection Wizard.

3. Follow the prompts in the Internet Connection Wizard and enter the information provided by your online service or Internet service provider.

Some online services send out zillions of free disks that help you sign up for their service; America Online is the best-known disk slinger out there. Just because you have a disk from AOL, however, it doesn't mean that you can use Outlook to read your mail from

AOL. You can still use the software you got from AOL to send and receive your mail on AOL, but you can't move mail messages from the AOL software's Personal Filing Cabinet to Outlook. AOL has announced plans to make AOL compatible with Outlook by mid-1998. When that happens, AOL tech support can help you make AOL and Outlook work together smoothly.

Printing E-Mail Messages

 Printing your e-mail messages is a quaint but sometimes convenient way to deal with the messages you send and receive. Now and then you run across someone who won't read stuff from a screen; they accept only ink on paper. No kidding. There are bosses out there who even have assistants type up their voice mail messages; I've seen it. Someday those types will go the way of the dinosaur, and we'll read all our mail on little screens built into our sunglasses while we sit on the beach. Until then, you may need to print out your e-mail messages from time to time.

Printing an individual message

You can print the text of a message you're reading in Outlook by clicking the Print button on the toolbar. The print tool sends your message directly to the printer — without opening a print dialog box in order to offer you some choices about what kind of paper to print on or which printer to use (if you're using a network with more than one printer). To see your range of choices before you print, choose File➪Print (or press Ctrl+P). The principles of printing are the same in all Outlook modules, so *see also* the directions given in "Printing your calendar" in Part III for more details.

Printing a list of messages

You can print a list of messages while viewing the contents of your Inbox, Outbox, Sent Items folder, or any mail folder you create. Here's what to do while viewing the list you want to print:

1. Choose File➪Print (or press Ctrl+P) to open the Print dialog box.

2. Pick Table Style in the Print Style list.

3. Choose other print options, such as the number of copies, which pages to print, and so forth.

4. Click OK. Your messages are then printed.

Outlook prints whatever message titles are shown in the Information Viewer when you call up the Print command. If you're looking at the Unread Messages view, for example, only the unread messages are printed. To print your entire list of messages, you have to switch to a view that includes all your messages, such as Messages view.

Using and Choosing E-Mail Views

One of the real benefits of Outlook is the variety of ways in which you can sort and arrange your collection of messages, as well as the several different ways you can look at what's in your messages. Your Outlook folders can serve as your filing system as well as your electronic mailbox.

You have many different arrangements you can use to view your e-mail messages. If you don't like the view you've got, you can choose View⇨Current View and pick a new view:

♦ *Messages* view is a plain vanilla list of your messages. The titles of unread messages are shown in boldface, whereas messages you've read are shown in a normal typeface.

✦ *Messages with AutoPreview* shows you the first few lines of all your unread messages.

✦ *By Follow-Up Flag* view shows a list of your messages according to what kind of flag you've assigned to each message.

✦ *Last Seven Days* view is a list of messages you've received within the last seven days.

✦ *Flagged for Next Seven Days* view shows only flagged messages with due dates scheduled within the next week.

✦ *By Conversation Topic* organizes your messages by subject.

✦ *By Sender* view groups your messages according to who sent the message.

✦ *Unread Messages* view shows only unread messages. After you read a message, this view no longer appears.

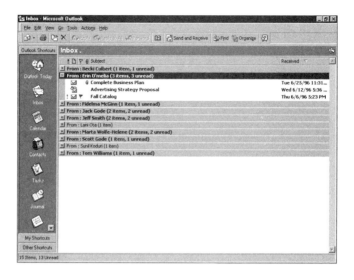

✦ *Sent To* view sorts messages according to the name of the person it's sent to. In your Inbox, most messages are sent to you, so it makes little sense to use this view in the Inbox. In your Sent Items folder, however, you can use the Sent To view to organize your outgoing messages according to the person to whom each message is sent.

✦ *Message Timeline* view shows you a diagram with your messages organized by the time they were sent or received. You can click the icon shown for any message and see that message.

The Calendar

There's never enough time in the day, so there's no sense wasting precious minutes figuring out what to do next. The Microsoft Outlook Calendar can help you organize appointments, holidays, and recurring events. You can also get Outlook to remind you about a meeting early enough to be sure that you get there on time.

In this part . . .

- ✔ **Making and changing appointments**
- ✔ **Finding a date**
- ✔ **Printing your calendar**
- ✔ **Viewing your schedule**

About Calendar

There's no big trick to using the Outlook calendar. If you've ever jotted an appointment in your FiloFax or on your *DOS For Dummies* desk calendar, you know how to cope with a calendar. The Outlook calendar is easier to change and share with other people on your office computer network than a regular paper calendar, but the basic concepts haven't changed since the Romans, so don't worry.

Accessing the Date Navigator

Outlook enables you to choose from several calendar styles. Some styles show you a bigger calendar with fewer dates, and some styles show a smaller calendar with more dates but include no notes about what's scheduled on a certain date. The Date Navigator is a small calendar that enables you to see your schedule for the date of your choice simply by clicking the date with your mouse. To use the Date Navigator:

1. Switch to the Calendar module by clicking the Calendar icon in the Outlook Bar to make your Calendar appear.

2. Choose View➪Current View➪Day/Week/Month.

3. Click either the Day, Work Week, or Week button on the toolbar.

The little three-month calendar in the upper-right corner is the Date Navigator. The rest of the screen shows you the appointments for the current week (or the days you've clicked in the Date Navigator). To see what's scheduled for a different date, just click the date on the Date Navigator.

Adding an Appointment

Outlook gives you lots of choices for entering details about your appointments, but you need to enter only two things: what and when. Everything else is optional.

If you want to schedule two appointments at the same time, Outlook subtly warns you with a banner at the top of the form that says `Conflicts with another appointment,` but nothing stops you from scheduling yourself to be in two places at once. Just to be safe, look at the schedule for the time you are scheduling first (see the preceding section, "Accessing the Date Navigator").

1. Click the Calendar icon in the Outlook Bar if you're not in the Calendar.

2. Click the New Appointment button in the toolbar.

3. Click in the Subject box and enter something there to help you to remember what the appointment is about.

4. Click in the Location box and enter the location, if you want. If you know the location, enter it here so that you don't forget.

5. In the Start Time boxes, enter the date and time when the appointment begins.

6. In the End Time boxes, enter the date and time when the appointment ends. If you ignore the End Time boxes, Outlook creates a 30-minute appointment.

7. If you want Outlook to remind you of your appointment, click the Reminder box.

8. Enter a category of your choice in the Categories box.

9. Click the Save and Close button in the toolbar.

If you're on a network and you don't want others to know about your appointment, click the Private box in the lower-right corner of the dialog box.

Adding an Event

An *event* is a type of Calendar entry that is a lot like an appointment, except that it lasts all day and isn't associated with a particular hour of the day. Holidays are events. You can schedule more than one event for the same day; for example, if your birthday falls on Christmas day, you can schedule two events for December 25. (You still only get one present, however.) You can also schedule a convention or business trip as an event and then continue scheduling appointments on the event day. Events also look different on your calendar: Each event appears as a gray banner on the calendar day on which it's scheduled.

You use exactly the same steps to enter events that you use to enter appointments, except that you also check the All Day Event box (see also "Adding an Appointment" earlier in this part.)

Adding Regularly Scheduled (Recurring) Appointments

Some appointments keep coming back like a bad penny. Your Monday morning staff meeting or Wednesday night bowling league roll around every week unchanged (except for your bowling score), so why enter the appointment over and over? Just call it a recurring appointment.

Creating a recurring appointment

To create a recurring appointment, follow these steps:

1. Click the New Appointment icon on the left end of the toolbar to open the New Appointment form.

2. Click in the Subject box and enter the subject.

3. Click in the Location box and enter the location.

4. Click the Recurrence button in the toolbar (or press Ctrl+G) to make the Recurrence box appear.

5. Click the Start text box and enter the starting time.

6. Click the End text box and enter the ending time. (Don't worry about the Duration box; Outlook calculates the duration for you. On the other hand, you can just enter the duration and let Outlook fill in the missing end time.)

7. In the Recurrence pattern box, click the Daily, Weekly, Monthly, or Yearly option button to select how often the appointment recurs.

8. In the next part of the Recurrence pattern box, choose how often the appointment occurs. The Recurrence pattern looks different depending on whether you chose Daily, Weekly, Monthly, or Yearly in Step 7. The preceding figure shows the Weekly Recurrence pattern box.

 - If you chose a Yearly pattern, choose something like the first Friday in February.

 - If you chose a Weekly recurrence pattern, choose something like every Tuesday.

- If you chose a Daily pattern, choose something like every eighth day.

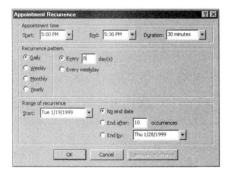

9. In the Range of Recurrence box, enter the first occurrence in the Start box.

10. Choose when the appointments will end. If you want the appointment to repeat indefinitely, you don't have to do anything; No End Date is checked by default if you don't choose something else. Don't worry about the box labeled End after 10 Occurrences; the button with the dot in it tells you what choice you've picked. After you create a recurring appointment with no end date, your appointment recurs forever until you reopen the Appointment form and change the pattern or delete the appointment.

11. Click OK.

12. Click Save and Close (or press Alt+S).

TIP

A quick way to enter the date when a recurring appointment will end is to enter something like **two years from now** and let Outlook translate that into an actual date.

Editing a recurring appointment

Outlook treats recurring appointments a wee bit differently than single appointments, because what you do to one appointment in a series of recurring appointments may affect later occurrences of that appointment. For example, if you change your regular Wednesday night tennis match to Thursday night in order to compete against players who are weaker or better looking (or both), you're probably changing all your future tennis dates. If you're just changing your match one Wednesday night in order to see your kid's school play, you're just changing one appointment in a series.

1. Double-click the appointment you want to change. The Open Recurring Item dialog box appears.

2. Choose whether you want to change just the occurrence you clicked or change the whole series.

3. Click OK to reopen the Appointment form.

4. Change the Date, Start time, the Recurrence pattern or any other details of the appointment in the Appointment form, just as you first entered the appointment (see the section "Adding an Appointment").

5. Click Save and Close (or press Alt+S).

You can still change individual occurrences of a recurring appointment by dragging the appointment to a different time. When you do, Outlook asks you `Change only this occurrence?` If you want to change only one occurrence, click OK.

Deleting an Appointment

Deleting items in Outlook is very intuitive, which means that you probably can figure out how to do it without my telling you. Of course, I'll tell you anyway.

1. Click the appointment that you want to delete.

2. Click the Delete button in the toolbar (or press Delete).

If you want to delete several appointments at once, hold down the Ctrl key while clicking each appointment you want to delete. Then press Delete.

Finding a Date

The Calendar in Outlook can schedule appointments hundreds or even thousands of years from now. In case you're concerned, Outlook has no problem with the year 2000 (or the year 3000 or 4000, for that matter). Because there are so many years to work with, you need a quick way to make the Calendar show the date you're thinking about. Here's the quick way:

1. Click the Calendar icon in the Outlook Bar, if you're not in the Calendar. When you switch to the Calendar module from another module, Outlook always shows you the current date.

2. Choose View➪Current View➪Day/Week/Month.

3. Choose Go➪Go to Date (or press Ctrl+G).

4. Enter the date you want, such as **12/25/2098**, or **Christmas 2098**, or **1 year from now**, or even **100 years from now**. Outlook figures out what you mean.

5. Click OK to make the Calendar display the date you've chosen.

 6. Click the Go to Today button in the toolbar to return to today's date.

Printing Your Appointments from Outlook

You may want to print a copy of your schedule to carry around as a reminder, or you can print your appointments for someone else to use. Outlook can print your appointment calendar in dozens of different formats to fit your preference.

If you currently use a paper planner and want to manage your schedule with Outlook and print it out to use in your paper planner, you can create pages that fit in several popular planners, including

✦ Day Timer

✦ Day Runner

✦ Franklin Day Planner

✦ FiloFax

You also can print a tiny copy of your schedule that's small enough to carry around in your billfold or a full-page calendar to post on a wall.

About the Print dialog box

When you click the print button on the toolbar (or press Ctrl+P), Outlook prepares to print a copy of whatever is on the screen by opening the Print dialog box. The Print dialog box changes the way it looks depending on which Outlook module you're using, what view you've chosen, and which items in the view you've selected (if any).

The Print Style list in the Print dialog box shows you a collection of tiny diagrams of different ways you can have your information arranged on the page. Click the diagram that looks the way you want your page to look.

Print Style button   ┌Page Setup box

Print Range box   Preview button

Define Styles button

The Page Setup button next to the Print Style box enables you to tell Outlook what kind of paper to use and other details about printing in the style you've chosen. Choices you make after clicking the Page Setup button apply only to the style you selected from the Print Style list.

The Define Styles button enables you to create your own styles and give each new style a name of your choice. After you create a style, the name and a diagram of the style appear in the Print Style list.

The Print Range box enables you to tell Outlook how much information to include on the pages you print. In the Calendar, you need to enter a range of dates. In all the other Outlook modules, you choose All Rows or Only Selected Rows.

The Preview button enables you to see exactly what your pages will look like when you print them. You'll save a lot of time if you preview your pages before printing them, because you can be sure that your pages look the way you want before wasting time and paper on printed copies. Previewing takes only a second.

About Print Styles

Each style that you see in the Print Styles list gives you a different collection of choices about what appears on the page you print. You may want to create entirely new styles to fit your needs. Perhaps you print a copy of your calendar every month to post on your wall, and another monthly calendar to carry around in your date book. You can create special styles for each and save the trouble of having to enter all the particulars about each calendar's paper size, paper type, page layout, and so forth every month.

To create a new Print style:

1. Click the Print button in the toolbar (or press Ctrl+P) to open the Print dialog box.

2. In the Print dialog box, choose Daily, Weekly, or Monthly from the Print Style list.

3. Click the Define Styles button to open the Define Styles dialog box.

4. Choose the style upon which you want to base your new style.

5. Click the Copy button to open the Page Setup dialog box.

6. Click the Style Name text box and enter the name you want to give your new style.

7. Choose the options you desire from the Format tab, including layout. The options that are available to you depend on the style that you chose as a basis for your new style in Step 4.

8. Click the Paper tab in the Page Setup dialog box.

9. From the Type list, choose the type of paper you're using.

10. From the Size list, choose the size of paper you're using.

11. If you want any particular information to print at the top or bottom of the page, click the Header/Footer tab and enter what you want to print.

12. Click the Print Preview button to see what your new style looks like.

13. Click OK to close the Page Setup dialog box.

14. Click Close to close the Define Print Styles dialog box.

15. Click OK to print your schedule.

After you define a style, its name shows up in the Print Styles list in the Print dialog box, so you only have to choose your style and click OK.

If you plan to print in a certain style only once, you don't need to create a whole new style; just click the Page Setup button and change the style to meet your needs.

Basic printing

If you've ever printed anything with Windows, you already know the basics: Put what you want to print on the screen and tell Outlook to print it. More choices are available when printing your calendar, but here's the basic method:

1. Click a date within the range of dates you want to print.

2. Click the Print button on the toolbar (or press Ctrl+P) to open the Print dialog box.

3. In the Print Style group, choose Daily, Weekly, Monthly, Trifold, Memo, or any other style you want that may be available in your Print Style box (see the preceding section, "About Print Styles").

4. In the Print Range box, set the range of dates you want to print.

5. Click OK.

Creating a billfold-sized calendar

One handy Calendar style is a tiny billfold-sized calendar that contains your schedule, a convenience calendar, and a list of your tasks.

Here's how to create a Billfold calendar that you can use every day:

1. Click the Calendar icon in the Outlook Bar, if you're not in the Calendar.

2. Choose View⋄Current View⋄Day/Week/Month.

3. Click either the Day, Work Week, or Week button in the toolbar.

4. Click the Print button in the toolbar (or press Ctrl+P) to open the Print dialog box.

5. In the Print dialog box, choose Trifold from the Print Style list.

6. Click the Page Setup button to open the Page Setup dialog box.

7. Click the Paper tab in the Page Setup dialog box.

8. Click Billfold from the Size list.

9. Click OK to close the Page Setup dialog box.

10. Click OK to print your schedule.

 The Billfold style prints your schedule in an area about the size of a dollar bill; so if you print on normal-sized paper, you have to take a pair of scissors and cut off the excess.

Planner-sized printing

If you're printing pages of your calendar to use in a planner book, such as Day Runner or Franklin Day Planner, you can take advantage of some of the print styles that come with Outlook. Here's how to set up your pages for a commercial planner:

1. Click the Calendar icon in the Outlook Bar, if you're not in the Calendar.

2. Choose View⇨Current View⇨Day/Week/Month.

3. Click the Print button in the toolbar (or press Ctrl+P) to open the Print dialog box.

4. In the Print dialog box, choose Daily, Weekly, or Monthly from the Print Style list.

5. Click the Define Styles button to open the Define Print Styles dialog box.

6. Click the Edit button to open the Page Setup dialog box.

7. Click the Paper tab in the Page Setup dialog box.

8. From the Type list, choose the type of paper you're using.

You can buy special paper for most types of planners from the people who manufacture the planners. If you're using paper from the original manufacturer, such as Day Runner or Franklin Day Planner, choose Custom in the Type list.

Avery also makes filler paper that fits some popular planners. Look for it at your local office supply store. If you're using Avery paper, choose the Avery paper type that's listed in the Type list.

9. Choose the type of planner for which you're printing pages (such as Day Runner Running Mate or Franklin Day Planner) in the Page Size list.

10. Click OK to close the Page Setup dialog box.

11. Click Close to close the Define Print Styles dialog box.

12. Click OK to print your schedule.

After you set up the page using the Define Print Styles dialog box, you get the same type of page every time you print your schedule.

Wall calendar printing

You can also create a calendar that fills a whole sheet of paper suitable for hanging on your wall or taping to the fridge. You can use paper as large as $8^{1}/_{2}$-by-14-inch legal paper. Here's what you do:

1. Click the Calendar icon in the Outlook Bar, if you're not in the Calendar module.

2. Choose View⇨Current View⇨Day/Week/Month.

3. Click the Print button in the toolbar (or press Ctrl+P) to open the Print dialog box.

4. In the Print dialog box, choose Daily, Weekly, or Monthly from the Print Style list.

5. Click the Page Setup button to open the Page Setup dialog box.

6. Click the Paper tab in the Page Setup dialog box.

7. Choose the paper size you're using from *both* the Type and Size lists (either Letter or Legal).

8. Click OK to close the Page Setup dialog box.

9. Click OK to print your schedule.

You have literally hundreds of combinations of paper sizes, styles, and layouts to use for printing your calendar. You can't hurt anything by experimenting with different sizes and trying new things.

Currently, you can't print a 6- or 12-month calendar on a single page in Outlook. It seems like a simple thing, but Outlook isn't up to that just yet.

Rescheduling an Appointment

Sometimes, the best-made appointments just won't stay the same. Outlook gives you several ways to change appointments.

Changing an appointment using drag and drop

Changing the starting time of an appointment is just a matter of using the drag-and-drop technique. Follow these steps to pick up the appointment and slide it to the date or time that you want.

1. Click the appointment in the Calendar view.

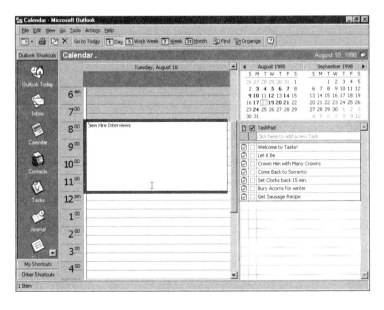

2. Place the mouse pointer over the blue bar; the mouse pointer turns into a little four-headed arrow.

3. Press the mouse button, drag the appointment to the new time or date, and release the button.

If you want to change the date of an appointment but not the time, it's easiest if you choose a view of your calendar that includes both the original appointment date and the date that you want to assign to the appointment. For example, to change the time, switch to the One-Day view and slide the appointment to its new time slot. To change an appointment to a date later in the same month, choose the 31-Day view and drag the appointment to the new date. Of course, you always can double-click the appointment to open it and then change everything (see the following section, "Reopening the appointment to change it").

Reopening the appointment to change it

Drag-and-drop isn't the ticket for changing appointment times when you can't view enough of the Calendar to see both the original date and the rescheduled date. In that case, all you can do is reopen the appointment and change the particulars by following these steps:

1. Double-click the appointment.

2. Click in the first Start Time block and enter the date you want to assign to your appointment.

3. Press the Tab key and enter the new appointment time in the text box (if you have a new time).

4. If necessary, make any other changes in the appointment by clicking the information you want to change and entering the revised information over it.

5. Click Save and Close (or press Alt+S).

Shortening or lengthening an appointment

When you're looking at the one-day view of your calendar, your appointments are shown as boxes of different sizes, depending on the length of the appointment. If you want to shorten or lengthen an appointment, just use your mouse to drag the border of the box that represents the appointment to make the appointment smaller or bigger.

Here's how to shorten or lengthen an appointment:

1. Click the appointment.

2. Move the mouse pointer over the line at the bottom of the appointment.

3. Drag the bottom line down to make the appointment time longer; drag the bottom line up to make the appointment shorter.

Another method is to drag the top line up or down, but bear in mind that dragging the top line changes both the appointment's length *and* its starting time.

Dragging the box to change the length of an appointment is the easiest way to go if all your appointments begin and end on the hour and half-hour. If your appointments don't start on the hour or half-hour, you can fine-tune the length of an appointment by opening the appointment and typing the starting and ending times you want (see also the following section, "Shortening appointments to less than 30 minutes").

You also can use the drag-and-drop method when you change the length of events. To change the length of an event, click the 31-Day button to switch to the Monthly view of your calendar and then just drag the line at the left or right end of the banner that represents an event to make an event longer or shorter.

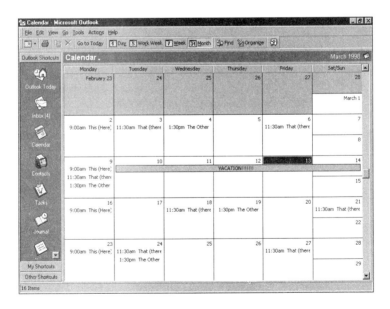

Shortening appointments to less than 30 minutes

When you use the drag-and-drop method to change the length of appointments, you can make appointments begin and end only on the hour and at 30 minutes after the hour. When you have appointments that you need to begin and end at other times, you have to open the appointment and enter the times you want, just as you did when you first created the appointment, like this:

1. Double-click the appointment.

2. To change the time the appointment starts, click the Start Time box and type the time you want.

3. To change the time the appointment ends, click the End Time box and type the time you want. You also can change any other details about the appointment that you want while the Appointment form is open.

4. Click Save and Close (or press Alt+S).

 Remember, when you enter times in Outlook, you don't have to be particular about punctuation. For example, when you type **5p**, Outlook understands that to be 5:00 p.m. and automatically converts the time to the proper format. Dates are even easier to enter; just enter **next Wed**, and Outlook converts that to the date.

Sharing Your Calendar

The only thing that wastes more time than going to meetings is calling people to find out when they can go to meetings. Outlook 98 enables you to share your calendar with other Outlook 98 users so that you can settle on a meeting time by checking another person's calendar yourself. You need to install an option called Net Folders from the Outlook 98 CD-ROM in order to share your Outlook folders with someone else. If you want to know more about sharing folders with Outlook 98, see the large, luxurious version of this book, *Microsoft Outlook 98 for Dummies,* which features a whole chapter devoted to Net Folders.

Viewing Appointments

You enter appointments in Outlook so that you can remember them later. In order to use your appointment list that way, you have to at least look at your list of appointments. Outlook enables you to view your list in dozens of ways (an Outlook view is a way of presenting information in the arrangement you need). Outlook comes with six different views, and you can create your own views as well. The following sections describe the views you get the very first time you use Outlook.

Basic Calendar views

When you first use Outlook, you have a half-dozen preprogrammed views from which to choose. You can add views to your heart's content in any Outlook module (see "Saving and deleting created views" in Part V), but you can go a long way with the views that Outlook starts with. Here's the lineup:

✦ *Day/Week/Month* view looks like a calendar. It has buttons in the toolbar to enable you to choose between viewing your appointments for one day, a week, or a whole month. You'll probably use this view more often than any other.

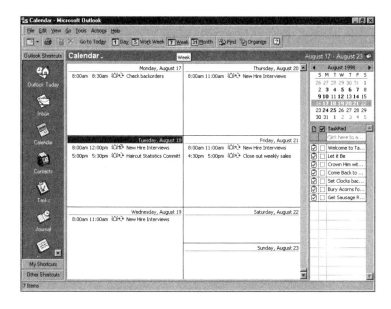

✦ *Active Appointments* is a list of appointments that are coming up in the near future. The Active Appointments view shows some of the same appointments as the Day/Week/Month view. The Active Appointments view, however, also shows you information about each appointment and enables you to sort the list according to the location or subject that you entered when you created the appointment.

✦ *Events* view is a list that shows you only items that you've
   designated as All day Events (see "Adding an Event" in this part).

✦ *Annual Events* view shows only the list of events that you've
   made into recurring events that happen yearly (see "Creating
   a recurring appointment" and "Adding an Event" in this part).
   You can enter holidays and anniversaries as annual events.

✦ *Recurring Appointments* lists all appointments and events that
   you've set as recurring appointments.

✦ *By Category* view groups your appointments according to the
   category you've assigned to each appointment. Grouped
   views work the same way in all Outlook modules (see "Using
   grouped views" in Part V).

Another popular way to view your upcoming appointments is to
click the Outlook Today icon in the Outlook Bar. As the name
suggests, Outlook Today pulls together everything you're doing
today — appointments, tasks, and messages — and displays it all
on a single page. You can print your Outlook Today page by
clicking the print icon on the toolbar or by pressing Ctrl+P.

Customizing the TaskPad

The Day/Week/Month view of your calendar includes a snippet of your Task list (see also Part IV). The TaskPad shows the very same items that you see if you switch to the Tasks module, but the information you see is less detailed. I find it handy to have the TaskPad available when I'm looking at my calendar so that I can view the things that I have to do at certain times as well as the things I can do anytime. Another benefit of the TaskPad is that, when I print my calendar, I also can print my tasks.

You can view or print tasks from the Calendar, but you can't view or print Calendar items from the Tasks module. If you need to view and print both at the same time, stay in the Calendar module.

You can set up the TaskPad to show your tasks in several ways. Here's how to choose the TaskPad style you prefer:

1. Click the Calendar icon in the Outlook Bar, if you're not in the Calendar module.

2. Choose View⇨Current View⇨Day/Week/Month.

3. Choose View⇨TaskPad View and pick the type of TaskPad view you want. The TaskPad uses the same views as the Tasks module (see also Part IV).

Resizing parts of the Day/Week/Month view

The one- and seven-day views in the Day/Week/Month view fill the screen with three parts that you can resize by dragging the borders with your mouse.

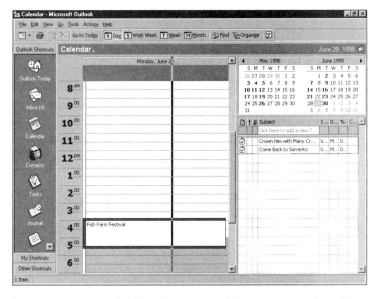

If you want to give the Date Navigator a bit more space, drag the gray borderline just below or to the left of the Date Navigator until it's the size you want. You can make the Date Navigator take up the whole screen if you want.

Dragging the border to the left of the TaskPad changes the amount of space that the TaskPad occupies. When you change the size of one element of the Day/Week/Month view, the other elements resize or disappear to compensate.

Tasks

All those little tasks I have to do every day have a way of slipping off my radar screen until just after I need to do them. That's why I like having a simple tool for tracking what needs to be done and when. The Tasks module enables me to deal with simple things quickly, yet it's designed to help me keep track of fairly complex activities.

You also can use Outlook to manage tasks in cooperation with your colleagues at work. In order to do that, however, your company must be running another Microsoft program, called Microsoft Exchange Server. I don't know whether your company uses Microsoft Exchange Server, so I don't want to confuse you. Therefore, I minimize the discussion of features that require Microsoft Exchange Server, such as responding to task requests and sending status reports. You get plenty of mileage out of the Outlook Tasks module by itself.

In this part . . .

- ✔ **Entering tasks**
- ✔ **Managing tasks**
- ✔ **Printing and viewing tasks**

Creating and Modifying Tasks

Outlook can handle all kinds of highfalutin information and details about each task you enter. I find that 90 percent of the time, I just need to type a quick note to jog my memory. For the other 10 percent, however, I need to go whole hog and keep lots of information handy about tasks I must do — things like travel directions, discussion notes, and so on.

Creating a task the quick, simple way

Most times, I need only a word or two to jog my memory about a task, something like **Call Mom.** I don't need a lot of detailed information about how to do that, so I resort to the fast way.

1. Click the Tasks icon on the Outlook Bar to switch to the Tasks module if you aren't already there.

If you don't see anything that says Click Here to Add a New Task, switch to a different view of your Task list by choosing View➪Current View➪Simple List (*see* "Choosing a view" in Part V).

2. Click the text that says Click Here to Add a New Task. Doing so makes an insertion point (a flashing vertical bar) appear where the words were.

3. Type the name of your task.

4. Press the Enter key to make your new task drop down to join your list of other tasks.

If you're using the Calendar, you can use a miniature version of the Task list, called the TaskPad. You can enter tasks in the TaskPad by typing in the box labeled Click Here to Add a New Task (*see* "Customizing the TaskPad" in Part III).

Creating a task the slow, complete way

Suppose that you need to enter more information about your task, such as driving directions, or you want to have Outlook remind you just before the task is due. There is no limit to the information you can add to a task if you go the slow, complete way.

Most of the steps I show you include an "If" to let you know that you can skip the step if you're not interested in saving the type of information it discusses. The only essential element of a task is the name of the task. Everything else is optional.

1. Click the Tasks icon on the Outlook Bar to switch to the Tasks module if you're not already there.

2. Click the New Task button on the toolbar (or press Ctrl+N) to open a blank New Task form.

3. Type the name of the task in the Subject box.

4. If you want to assign a due date to the task, click the Due Date button; then click the Due Date box and enter the due date. You don't have to be too fussy about how you enter the date; Outlook understands **7/4/98, the first Saturday of July,** or **90 days from today** — however you like it.

5. If you want to enter a start date, click the Start Date box and enter a date. Not all tasks have start dates, so you can skip this step if you want.

6. If you want to keep track of the status of a task, click the triangle at the right end of the Status box (the scroll-down button). You have to revise your task as the status of the task progresses (*see* "Modifying a task the quick, simple way" later in this part).

7. If the task you're entering is unusually important, urgent, or even relatively unimportant, click the scroll-down button at the right end of the Priority box to choose the priority of the task.

8. If you want to be reminded before the task is due, click the Reminder check box and then click the date box next to it and enter the date when you want to be reminded. Enter the time of day when you want to activate the reminder in the time box.

9. If you want, enter miscellaneous notes and information about this task in the text box.

10. If you want to assign a category to your task, type the category you desire in the Categories text box.

11. Click the Save and Close button (or press Alt+S) to finish.

You can enter quite a lot of detailed information if you use the slow, complete method, but you don't have to use this method all the time. Another advantage of the slow, complete method is that you can use it to create a task when you're using any other Outlook module; just press Ctrl+Shift+K to open the New Task form and then start on Step 3.

Modifying a task the quick, simple way

If you entered a task the simple way (*see* the earlier section "Creating a task the quick, simple way"), you can change the task just as easily if you're viewing the same list. You can change any information that you see in any view (*see* "Choosing a view" later in this part). It's this easy:

1. Click the item that you want to change.

2. Select the old information by highlighting it.

3. Type the new information.

4. Press the Enter key.

You can change any information you can see in any view of the Tasks module other than the Timeline view. For more on Outlook views in general, *see* "Choosing a view" in Part V.

Modifying a task the slow, complete way

You can use the same method to change the information in a task that you used to enter the information in the first place. Although this slow, complete method requires a little more effort, you can enter much more precise information.

1. If you're not already in the Tasks module, go to it by clicking the Tasks icon in the Outlook Bar.

2. Choose View⇨Current View⇨Simple List.

3. To open the Task form, double-click the name of the task that you want to change.

4. If you want to change the name of the task, click your mouse in the Subject text box and type a different name.

5. If you want to change the due date, click the Due Date box and enter the new due date.

6. If you want to change the start date, click the Start Date box and enter the new start date.

7. If you want to change the status of a task, click the scroll-down button at the right end of the Status box. A menu appears that enables you to choose a different status.

8. If you want to choose a different priority level for a task, click the scroll-down button at the right end of the Priority box and choose your priority: low, medium, or high. If you leave the priority marking alone, your task will be marked as Normal.

9. If you want to turn the reminder on or off, click the Reminder check box.

10. If you want to enter or change the date when you want to be reminded, click the date box next to the Reminder check box; change the time you want to activate the reminder in the time box. Changing the reminder time is optional.

11. If you want to add or change miscellaneous notes and information about the task, click the text box at the bottom of the form and make whatever changes you want.

12. Click the Save and Close button (or press Alt+S) to finish.

I use only the slow, complete way of changing Task information about 10 percent of the time, because I'm too impatient to fill out a whole Task form. It's really not that much trouble, though.

Creating Recurring Tasks

When tasks have to be done over and over on a regular schedule, set them up as *recurring* tasks. You can designate a task as recurring while you're entering the task the first time.

You also can create a recurring task by reopening the task and following these steps:

1. Double-click the task to open the Task form.

 2. To open the Task Recurrence dialog box, click the Recurrence button located on the toolbar of the Task form (or press Ctrl+G).

3. Choose the <u>D</u>aily, <u>W</u>eekly, <u>M</u>onthly, or <u>Y</u>early option to specify how often the task occurs.

4. In the next box to the right, specify how often the appointment occurs, such as **every third day** or **the first Monday of each month.**

5. In the Range of Recurrence area, enter the first occurrence in the <u>S</u>tart box.

6. Choose when the appointments will stop (no end date, after a certain number of occurrences, or at a certain date).

7. Click OK to close the Task Recurrence dialog box.

8. Click <u>S</u>ave and Close (or press Alt+S).

Recurring tasks can be confusing, because the Task Recurrence dialog box changes appearance depending on whether you chose a Daily, Weekly, Monthly, or Yearly recurrence pattern. The principles for creating a recurring task are the same as those you use for creating recurring appointments. For more information, *see* "Adding regularly scheduled (recurring) appointments" in Part III.

Creating Regenerating Tasks

Sometimes it doesn't make sense to schedule the next occurrence of a task until you've actually completed the preceding occurrence. For example, if you get your hair cut every two weeks, but you get busy and get one haircut a week late, you still want to wait two weeks for the following haircut. If you use Outlook to schedule your haircuts, set it up as a regenerating task. (If only I could get Outlook to make my hair regenerate as well.) A regenerating task would be "getting a haircut every two weeks" while a recurring task is "getting a haircut every Monday."

1. Double-click the task to open the Task form.

 2. Click the Recurrence button on the toolbar in the Task form (or press Ctrl+G) to open the Task Recurrence dialog box.

3. Click the Regenerate New Task option.

4. Enter the number of months between regenerating the task.

5. Click OK to close the Task Recurrence dialog box.

6. Click Save and Close (or press Alt+S).

 I wish I could schedule tasks to regenerate every few days or every few weeks, but the only choice available in Outlook is to regenerate tasks in full-month increments.

Linking a Task to a Document or Other Item

You can include word-processing documents, spreadsheets, or any other type of file in a task by making the document an *attachment*. For example, if you've had a bad day and entered **Update Resume** as your new task, you can link your resume to the task to find the resume faster when you're ready to update it.

To link a task to an attachment, follow these steps:

1. Double-click the task to open the Task form.

 2. Click the Insert File tool on the toolbar to open the Insert File dialog box.

3. Choose the file you want to attach from the list of files in the Insert File dialog box.

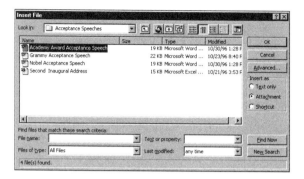

4. Click OK to close the dialog box and return to the Task form.

5. Click Save and Close (or press Alt+S).

The process of attaching files to your tasks is very much like the process for attaching files to your e-mail messages or any other Outlook item. For more about attaching files, *see* "Attaching files to your messages" in Part II. When you delete a task that has a file attached, the file is not deleted, only the task.

Managing Tasks

After you've entered tasks, you don't want to leave them hanging in the Task list forever. Change 'em, delete 'em, complete 'em, whatever; just don't let your tasks idly sit there! Managing your tasks is nearly as easy as entering them. The only bad thing about managing tasks is that you still have to do them; that's one problem that Outlook still can't solve.

Copying a task

You may have to perform the same task several times on different days — such as updating inventory. The fastest way to create a second copy of a task you've already entered is to copy the task.

To copy a task, follow these steps:

1. Select the task that you want to copy.

2. Choose Edit⇨Copy (or Ctrl+C).

3. Choose Edit⇨Paste (or Ctrl+V) where you want the copied task to appear.

Lo and behold, two identical tasks are now in your Task list. (I guess that there's *some* difference between the two — the date, the location, whatever.) To change details of one of the tasks, *see* the earlier section "Modifying tasks the slow, complete way" in this part.

Deleting a task

Sometimes you change your mind about a task that you've assigned yourself and want to delete the task. Deleting tasks is *so* much simpler than getting them done.

1. Select the task by highlighting it.

 2. Click the Delete button on the toolbar (or press Ctrl+D).

You'll never know the task existed.

Marking a task as complete

It's pretty satisfying to note your accomplishments for the day. You can do so by marking off each task as you add to the list of tasks you've finished, which you can also view. You can even send the boss a list of the tasks you've accomplished. First, however, you have to mark those tasks as complete (assuming that you've completed them, that is).

To mark a task as complete, follow these steps:

1. If you're not in the Tasks module, switch to it by clicking the Tasks icon on the Outlook Bar.

2. Choose View⟹Current View⟹Simple List.

3. Click the box next to the name of the task that you want to mark as complete.

Outlook puts a line through the names of tasks you've completed if you're viewing the Simple List. If you're using a different view, such as the Active Tasks view, your completed task vanishes entirely. To see only the tasks you've completed, use the Completed Tasks view. For more about views of your Task list, *see* "Choosing a view" later in this part.

Marking several tasks as complete

Maybe you're too busy to sit around marking tasks as complete; maybe you wait until the end of the day to mark off your completed tasks in one fell swoop.

To mark several tasks as complete, follow these steps:

1. If you're not in the Tasks module, switch to it by clicking the Tasks icon in the Outlook Bar.

2. Choose View⇨Current View⇨Simple List.

3. Click the first task that you want to mark.

4. Hold down the Ctrl key and then click each of the other tasks that you want to mark. The items you click turn blue to signify that you've selected them.

5. Right-click one of the tasks that you've highlighted to open the shortcut menu.

6. Choose Mark Complete.

All the tasks you selected appear with a check mark to show that they're completed. A line appears through the name of the task to drive the point home.

Sending a task to someone else

The quickest way to get a task out of your hair is to get someone else to do it. Outlook enables you to send tasks to your coworkers for completion. However, your office network must be set up to allow it. If you're using Outlook on an office network that uses Microsoft Exchange Server, you can see status information entered by the person to whom you assigned the task. If your office network isn't set up to enable you to assign tasks (or if you're not on an office network), tasks you assign to others are received as e-mail messages.

To assign a task to someone else, follow these steps:

1. Double-click the task you want to assign to someone else.

 2. Click the Assign Task button on the toolbar to open the Task form.

3. Type the name of the person to whom you want to assign the task in the To box. (This step presumes that you've already set up the person's name and e-mail address in your Contact list. If you haven't, *see* Part V.)

4. Click Send (or press Alt+S).

The task then appears in your Task list with a special icon next to it. The icon tells you that you've assigned this task to someone else for completion. If the task went out as an e-mail message, the message appears in your Sent Items folder (*see* "Using the Sent Items folder" in Part II).

 Assigning a task is the same as telling someone what to do. If the person to whom you're sending the task isn't required to do things at your request, some hard feelings could arise if you haven't cleared the request with that person first, so use discretion.

Setting the color of overdue or completed tasks

When a task becomes overdue, Outlook changes the color of the task name from the normal black to an alarming red to get your attention. Each task that you've finished becomes gray with a line through it. If you prefer another way to display overdue and completed tasks, you can change it.

To change the color of overdue and completed tasks, follow these steps:

1. Choose Tools⇨Options to open the Options dialog box.

2. Click the Task Options button.

3. Click the scroll-down button at the right end of the Overdue Tasks box to see your choice of colors.

4. Choose a color for overdue tasks by clicking the color you desire.

5. Click the scroll-down button at the right end of the Completed Tasks box to see your choice of colors.

6. Choose a color for completed tasks.

7. Click OK.

The Options dialog box disappears, and your tasks appear in Living Blue or Marvelous Magenta (or whatever you chose).

Skipping a recurring task once

Now and then you may want to skip a task that you've scheduled but still want to keep the other occurrences of that task set up.

To skip a recurring task, follow these steps:

1. Double-click the name of the task that you want to skip. The Task form opens.

2. Choose Actions⇨Skip Occurrence.

3. Click Save and Close (or press Alt+S).

The due date of the task changes to the next scheduled due date for the task. Skipping one occurrence of a task leaves all the other occurrences unchanged.

Viewing and Printing Tasks

The Tasks module enables you to view what you print and to print what you view. A few embellishments are available, but that's pretty much the size of it: What you see is what you get. You can customize your views and then print the newly customized view just as you see it.

Choosing a view

Task lists are just that: lists of tasks. You don't typically need fancy layouts when you choose a view. You just need a list that contains the information you want. To switch between views, choose View⇨Current View, and then pick the view you want to use. Here are the views that come with Outlook right out of the box:

✦ *Simple List* view is just the facts: the names you gave each task and the due date you assigned (if you assigned one). The Simple List view makes it easy to add new tasks and to mark old ones as complete. However, you won't see any extra information.

✦ *Detailed List* view is a little more . . . uh, detailed than the Simple List view. It's really the same information, plus the status of the tasks, the percentage of each task complete, and whatever categories you may have assigned to your tasks.

✦ *Active List* view shows you only tasks that you haven't finished yet. After you mark a task as complete, zap! Completed tasks vanish from the Active List view, which helps keep you focused on the tasks remaining to be done.

✦ *Next Seven Days* view is even more focused than the Active List view. The Next Seven Days view shows only uncompleted tasks scheduled to be done within the next seven days. It's just right for those who like to live in the moment, or at least within the week.

✦ *Overdue Tasks* view shows (oops!) tasks you've let slip past the due date you assigned. You ought to finish these up before the boss finds out.

✦ *By Category* view breaks up your tasks according to the category that you've assigned each task. You can open and close categories in order to focus on the type of tasks you're looking for. For example, you may assign a category of Sales to the sales-related tasks in your list. When you want to focus on sales, use the By Category view and click the Sales category.

✦ *Assignment* view lists your tasks in order by the name of the person upon whom you've dumped . . . er, I mean, delegated each task.

✦ *By Person Responsible* view contains the same information as the Assignment view, but the list is grouped (*see* "Using grouped views" in Part V) so that you can see the assignments of only one person at a time.

✦ *Completed Tasks* view shows (you guessed it) only tasks you've marked as complete. You don't need to deal with completed tasks anymore, but looking at the list gives you a warm, fuzzy feeling, doesn't it?

✦ *Task Timeline* view draws a picture of when each task is scheduled to start and end. Seeing a picture of your tasks gives you a better idea of how to fit work into your schedule sensibly.

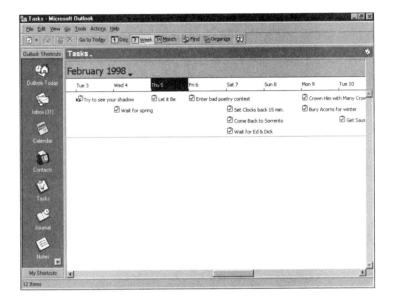

Printing a single task

After you've entered a task that includes lots of details about when, where, and how to do the task, you can print the task to give someone a copy or you can carry the copy around for your own reference.

Here's how you print a single task:

1. Click the name of the task to select it.

2. Click the Print icon on the toolbar to open the Print dialog box.

3. Choose Memo Style from the Print Style list.

4. If you want to print any document that you may have attached to your task, click the box that says Print Attached Files with Item(s). (For more information, *see* "Linking a Task to a Document or Other Item" earlier in this part.)

5. Click OK.

Bill Dyszel

Subject:	Review lease
Due Date:	Wednesday, December 03, 1997
Status:	In Progress
Percent Complete:	30%
Total Work:	2 hours
Actual Work:	1 hour
Owner:	Bill Dyszel
Categories:	Move

Be sure the lease includes

Heat
Garage space
Allowance for Signage
Indemnification
Cellar space

1

Now you can run to the printer and wait for your printed output to appear in Beautiful Living Black and White.

Printing a view

After you find a view that contains the information you want, printing that view is easy. You also can print the contents of each and every item.

To print a view, follow these steps:

1. Choose View⇨Current View and pick the view you want to print.

2. If you don't want to print every single item on the screen, select the ones you want to print by holding down the Ctrl key while clicking the tasks you want to print. The tasks you select are shaded blue to show that you've selected them. If you want to print all the items in the view, skip to the next step.

3. Click the Print icon on the toolbar to open the Print dialog box.

4. Choose Table Style from the Print Style list. The other choice, Memo Style, prints each task as a full page in full detail. Table Style printing looks a lot like the view you chose.

5. If you want to print everything in the view, choose All Rows in the Print Range box. If you selected certain tasks in Step 2 and want to print only those, choose Only Selected Rows.

6. Click OK.

Remember, your printed output includes only items that appear in the view you chose before you clicked the Print button. What you see is what you get.

Contacts

Outlook uses the word Contacts to mean people. I think that sounds sort of clandestine, but you may find it thrilling. Anyway, the Contact list is where you store people's names, addresses, phone numbers, and anything else you need to remember about the people in your life (maybe a code name?). You can collect a pretty formidable dossier on each person in your Contact list, including a dozen different phone numbers and any kind of free-form information. You also can use the Find feature to locate the information you've entered.

In this part . . .

- ✓ Adding names to your Contact list
- ✓ Finding contacts
- ✓ Viewing contacts
- ✓ Printing a Contact list

Adding Names, Numbers, and Other Stuff

In the Contacts module, you can save and organize nearly any type of information about the people you deal with. You then can find everything again lickety-split. If you like, you can enter quick scraps of information without interrupting the flow of your work (*see* "Adding a name the quick, simple way"). You also can spend the time to enter minutely detailed information every time you create a new contact.

Adding a name the quick, simple way

The quick, simple way of entering names into your Contact list may be a bit too limited: You simply can't enter all the information you may need. But at times, you need to save only a person's name, company, and phone number, so having a quick way to save this information is a good thing.

To enter names into your Contact list, follow these steps:

1. If you're not in the Contacts module, click the Contacts icon in the Outlook Bar.

2. Choose View⇨Current View⇨Phone List to reveal a simple list of names and addresses.

3. Click the first line of the Phone List. A message appears that says `Click here to enter a new Contact.` (Don't be alarmed if the message says only `Click here to enter a n . . . .` That's just what Outlook does when the column's too narrow. Just click anyway.) You can change the width of any column in any Outlook view by dragging the right border at the top of the column in the header row (*see* the section "Get the best fit" in Part VII).

4. Type the name of the person you want to enter in your Contact list.

5. Press Tab to move to the next column, labeled Company. Type the name of the company for which the person works.

6. Keep pressing Tab to move right one column at a time, and enter whatever information you want, including phone numbers, fax numbers, and categories.

7. After you're finished, press Enter to make your new contact drop down into the list with your other contacts.

If you want to enter more information, you always can reopen the item and change anything you want at another time. I find it quicker to get a name and phone number and then add the other stuff later.

Adding a name the slow, complete way

Adding names to your Contact list is as simple as filling out a form. You don't have to fill in everything the form asks for, just the name of the contact that you're entering. While you're entering the name, you may as well enter other things you need to know about the person, such as an address, phone number, e-mail address, Web page address, and whatever.

To add a name to your Contact list, follow these steps:

1. Click the Contacts icon in the Outlook Bar, if you're not already in the Contacts module.

2. Click the New Contact button on the toolbar. The New Contact form appears.

3. Enter the person's name In the Full Name box. When you open the New Contact Form, the insertion point is already in the Full Name text box, so you don't have to click anywhere. Enter the first name and then the last name, such as **George Washington.**

Outlook automatically figures which is the first name and which is the last name, and it makes sense of prefixes and suffixes like **Dr., Mr.,** and **Jr.** If you plan to use your Contact

list to create form letters in Microsoft Word, click the Full
Name button to see how Outlook dealt with the name. Outlook
gets it right more often than not, but if you see the first name
in the Middle name box or the last name in the Suffix box, you
can enter the correct names in the proper boxes.

When you enter a name in the Full Name text box, like **George
Washington,** and then press Tab or click your mouse in any
other box, the name appears again in the File As box — except
now the name appears last name first: Washington,
George. The entry in the File As box tells you how Outlook
plans to file your contact — in this case, by the last name, in
the W section. You also can file a contact according to some
other word. For example, George Washington could also be
filed under F for father of our country. More practical examples are filing the name of your plumber under the word
Plumber, your auto mechanic under Mechanic, and so on.

4. Click the Address box and enter the person's address. Outlook
interprets addresses using the same method it uses to make
sense of names. Breaking the address into street, city, state,
zip code, and country enables you to use the Outlook Contact
list as a source of addresses when creating form letters in
Microsoft Word. You don't have to do anything to make
Outlook perform this interpretation trick (*parsing,* as the
techies call it). But you may want to double-check the Outlook
interpretation by clicking the Address button. After you click
the Address button, the Check Address dialog box appears,
showing you how Outlook interpreted the address you
entered. If the name of the city wound up in the State/Province
box, or the name of the state wound up in the Zip Code box,
you can fix everything in the Check Address dialog box.

5. Click the check box labeled This Is the Mailing Address if the address you've just entered is the contact address to which you plan to send mail.

6. Click in the text box to the right of the Business phone box and type in the contact's business phone number.

7. Click in the text box to the right of the Home phone box and type in the contact's home phone number.

8. Click in the text box to the right of the E-mail address list box and enter your contact's e-mail address.

9. Click in the Web Page text box if the contact has a Web page. Enter the Uniform Resource Locator (URL), or Web address, for that page so that you can link to that page directly from the address card.

10. Click in the large text box at the bottom of the form and type in anything you want.

11. Click the <u>C</u>ategories button at the bottom-left of the screen to assign a category to the contact, if you like.

12. Click the name of each category that applies to your contact. If none of the existing categories suit you, click <u>M</u>aster Category List in the lower-right corner to see the Master Category list box.

13. Type the name of a new category in the <u>I</u>tem(s) Belong to These Categories box at the top of the Master Category list box.

14. Click Add and then click OK to return to the Categories list.

15. Click the name of the category you've just added, which now appears in the Categories list.

16. Click OK to close the Categories list and return to the New Contact form.

17. Click the Private box in the lower-right corner of the Contact form if you're on a network and you don't want others to know about your contacts. After you click it, you should see a check mark in the Private box that indicates it's turned on.

18. Click the Journal tab at the top left of the form to set your Journaling Preferences. The Journal page appears.

19. After you're finished, click Save and Close (or press Alt+S) to close the New Contact form.

With the help of Outlook, you easily can save and recall a huge list of items about all your contacts. Do as much or little as you like. You always can go back and make changes later.

AutoDialing

After you've entered the phone number for a contact, you don't
have to settle for just looking up that person's number; you can
make Outlook dial the number for you. You need to have a modem
attached to your computer and a phone attached to the modem
and, of course, you must already have the person's phone number
entered in the Phone list.

1. Click the Contacts icon in the Outlook Bar. Your Contact list
appears.

2. Click the name of the contact you want to call. The name is
highlighted to show which name you chose.

3. Choose Actions➪Call Contact and choose which of the
contact's phone numbers you want to dial. The New Call
dialog box appears.

4. If you want to create a Journal entry for the call, click the box
labeled Create New Journal Entry When Starting New Call. A
check mark appears in the check box.

5. If the number shown in the New Call dialog box is the number
you want to dial, click Start Call. If the contact has more than
one phone number, the first one that turns up in the New Call
dialog box may not be the one you want, so click the scroll-
down button next to the phone number and pick the number
you want; then click Start Call to see the Call Status dialog box.

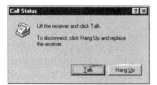

6. When the Call Status dialog box opens, pick up the phone.

7. When the person you're calling picks up the phone, click the
Talk button in the Call Status dialog box to make the Call
Status dialog box disappear.

8. After you finish the call, click the End Call button in the New Call dialog box. The phone hangs up when you click the End Call button.

9. Click the Close button to make the New Call dialog box disappear.

The main reason to use AutoDialing is so that you can keep records of how many phone calls you make, whom you call, and how long each call lasts. If you bill for your time, or just get reimbursed for phone calls, you'll be glad you have an easy way to track your phone calls.

Changing contact information

The main advantage to saving names and addresses with a program like Outlook is that, when the information you collect about the people you deal with changes over time, you can easily update your records.

Making changes to an item in your Contact list is simple. Just follow these steps:

1. Double-click the name of the contact you want to change. The contact item appears.

2. Click the information you want to change or click in the text box for the information you want to add. Type the new information.

3. Click Save and Close (or press Alt+S).

If you want to change information that you added from the Phone List view (*see* "Adding a name the quick, simple way" earlier in this part), just click the information you want to change in the Phone List view and enter the new information.

Finding Contacts

I assume that you want to find the names of your contacts sometime in the future, if you take the time to enter them in the first place. The quick, simple way to find a contact is simply to look up the name. Sometimes, however, you can't remember the name. You may recall something else about the person that you know you entered — such as the company that she works for or the city where he lives. The following sections show you several ways you can dig up information about your contacts.

Finding a contact the quick, simple way

The quick, simple way of finding a contact assumes that you remember the last name or the word that you used in the File As box.

To find a contact by last name, follow these steps:

1. Choose View⇨Current View⇨Address Cards (for more on choosing views, **see** "Choosing a view" later in this part). The Address Cards view looks like a deck of address cards laid out across your screen.

2. Type the first letter of the contact's last name. The view moves to that part of the Address Cards view that contains people whose names start with that letter.

3. If you still don't see the person's name, press the right arrow key to scroll through the list alphabetically.

If you entered something other than the contact's name in the File As box, such as Plumber or Dentist, type the letter **P** for Plumber or **D** for Dentist (**see also** "Adding a name the slow, complete way").

Finding a contact using the Advanced Find tool

You can use the Find tool in the toolbar to find a contact quickly the same way you find any other Outlook item (**see** "Finding a Note" in Part VI), but the Advanced Find tool can do a more detailed search if that's what you want. Sometimes you can't recall the name of the person you're looking for, but you remember some fragment of the information that you entered about them. For example, you remember that his name ends with Jr. Or you remember that she lives in Omaha. The Find Items tool finds all Items that contain the tiniest scrap of information you entered. Here's how to use the Find Items tool:

To search for a contact using the Advanced Find tool, follow these steps:

1. Choose Tools⇨Advanced Find (or press Ctrl+Shift+F) to open the Advanced Find dialog box.

2. Click the scroll-down button at the right end of the Look For text box.

3. Choose Contacts from the menu. If you start from the Contacts module, the Look For box should already say Contacts.

4. Click the triangle at the right end of the In text box under the Contacts tab setting to see the list of parts of the Contact list you can search.

5. Choose Frequently-Used Text Fields.

6. Click the Search for the Word(s) text box and enter the text you want to find.

7. Click the Find Now button. A little magnifying glass turns in circles while Outlook finds contact items that contain the text

you entered. When items are found, their names appear in a
list at the bottom of the Find Items dialog box.

8. Double-click the name of a contact in the list at the bottom of
the Find Items dialog box to see that person's Contact record.

After you open a Contact record located by the Find Items tool, the
Find Items dialog box remains open in the background, in case you
want to open another contact that turned up in your search. Just
click the icon on the Windows taskbar at the bottom of the
Contact Record screen that says Find – Contacts to return to the
Find Items dialog box. Press Esc to close the Find Items dialog box
after you're finished.

Viewing Contacts

You can look at your Contact list in a variety of views, just as you
can look at the information in all Outlook modules in a variety of
ways. If you spend a lot of time dealing with contacts, you can
save a lot of time using the options for sorting, grouping, and
filtering the different items in an Outlook view.

About views

Although Outlook comes with dozens of different views, and you
can create hundreds more if you like, Outlook really has only a

handful of basic view types. You can see what the choices are by choosing View⇨Current View⇨Define Views and then clicking the New button. (After you've finished looking, press Esc twice to return to the screen from where you started.)

If this list seems small, think of each type of view as if it were a type of recipe. Five types of recipes — appetizers, salads, soups, entrees, and desserts — can be the basis for an unlimited number of recipes. You can cook up an equally endless variety of views, beginning with these five general types. The Create a New View dialog box only enables you to choose among five basic types of view in any Outlook module:

✦ *Table* view is your plain vanilla arrangement of rows and columns. The Phone List view in the Contacts module, the Simple List in the Tasks module, and the Active Appointments view of the Calendar are all examples of table-type views.

✦ *Timeline* views draw a picture depicting each item in a view, either in order of their due dates or the date when you dealt with them. The Inbox, Tasks, and Journal modules all include Timeline views. No real need exists for a Timeline view of your Contact list, although you can create one (*see* "Saving and deleting created views" later in this part).

✦ *Card* views look like a collection of file cards. The Address Cards and Detailed Address Cards views in your Contacts module are the only examples of Card views that are included with Outlook.

✦ *Day/Week/Month* views are calendar-style views designed — you guessed it — for the Calendar module.

✦ *Icons* views fill the screen with icons representing each item and a title that matches the title of the item. The Notes module uses Icons views.

Choosing a view

Contact views come with Outlook when you first start the program. These views cover things for which most people use the Contact list. But you can add as many views as you need, so don't feel limited by the initial selection. Here's what you have when you begin:

✦ *Address Cards* is a view that looks like a screen full of little file cards arranged in alphabetical order. You only see a few key items in the Address Cards view, such as name, mailing address, phone number, and e-mail address.

♦ *Detailed Address Cards* is a more detailed version of the Address Cards view. This view shows everything on the first page of the Contact form, including the person's title, company, and the first few lines of text from the text box at the bottom of the Contact form.

♦ *Phone List* turns your collection of contacts into a plain-looking list of names, addresses, and phone numbers. The Phone List view is not as pretty as the Address Cards view or the Detailed Address Cards view. However, you can sort, group, and categorize your contacts in this view in ways that aren't possible in those other two views.

♦ *By Category* looks similar to the Phone List view, but the Category view does a trick called *grouping*. Contacts are clumped together according to the category you've assigned to each of them. Contacts not assigned a category are clumped into a category called None.

♦ *By Company* is similar to the By Category view: They are both grouped views (grouped views in Outlook usually have a name that starts with the word *By*). This view groups items according to the Company you've entered for each contact.

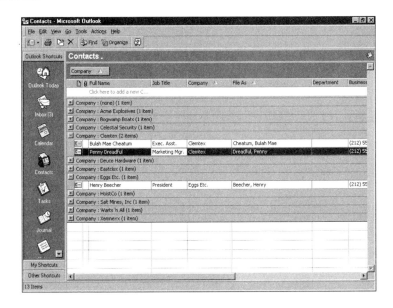

♦ *By Location* is like the other two *By* views. It gathers contacts together — in this case, according to the country that you've entered for each contact. I changed my By Location view to group by state, because I have very few contacts outside the United States. If you have contacts in many countries, however, you can leave the location setup alone.

♦ *By Follow-Up Flag* view shows a list of your messages according to what kind of flag you assigned to each message.

See "Saving and deleting created views" later in this part to see how to change a view to suit your needs and save it.

Switching between views in any Outlook module is as simple as changing channels on your TV. Choose <u>V</u>iew➪Current <u>V</u>iew and then pick the view you want. If you don't like the new view, just switch back by using the same commands to choose the view you were looking at before.

Filtering views

Filtered views show only items that have certain characteristics, such as a certain job title or a certain date. All views in all Outlook modules can be filtered, and some modules include filtered views. The Calendar module includes an Events view, which shows only items that are classified as Events (*see* "Viewing the Calendar" in Part III). The Tasks module has a view called Next Seven Days, which filters out all tasks except those whose due date falls within the next seven days (*see* "Choosing a view" in Part IV). When you're using a filtered view, the words Filter Applied appear in the Folder Banner just above the Information Viewer.

The Contacts module doesn't come with any filtered views when you begin using Outlook, but you can easily create filtered views of your Contact list if you want. Filtered views are useful if you frequently need to see a list of contacts who work at different companies but have the same job title, such as President or Sales Manager. You may also want to create a filtered view of contacts who live in your immediate vicinity if you need to call on customers in person. Use this process for filtering a view and then save the view (*see* "Saving and deleting created views" later in this part).

To filter items in a view, follow these steps:

1. Choose View➪Current View➪Edit Current View to open the View Summary dialog box.

2. Click the Filter button to open the Filter dialog box.

3. Enter the text that you want to filter in the box labeled Search for the Word(s). For example, if you want to see only the names of people whose job title is President, type the word **President** in the box.

4. Click the scroll-down button next to the In text box to reveal the list of field types you can choose from. I think that the In text box is organized in a weird way: You have to choose from some pretty vague categories, like Frequently-Used Text Fields and Name Fields. I don't find the choices very helpful. I have managed to find what I'm looking for most often when I choose Frequently-Used Text Fields.

5. Click OK to filter your list. The words Filter Applied appear in the Folder Banner, and your list shows only the items that match the text that you entered in Step 3.

The reason the words Filter Applied appear is to let you know that the view you're seeing shows only items that match some kind of filter. That's important to know, because you still can create new items while looking at a filtered view. If you create a new item that doesn't match the filter while looking at a filtered view, the item you create seems to disappear. For example, if you're using a filtered view that shows only the names of presidents of companies and you create a contact for someone whose job title is Sales Manager, that contact won't appear on a list filtered to show only presidents. To see Sales Managers, you have to switch to a view that shows everybody on the list, not just presidents.

Putting new fields in a view

Most Outlook views display fewer than a dozen fields, even though items in nearly every Outlook module can store several dozen fields. You can add fields to any Outlook view and use the fields you add to sort, group, or filter your collection of items.

To add a field to any Outlook view, follow these steps:

1. Choose View⇨Current View⇨Edit Current View to open the View Summary dialog box.

2. Click the Fields button. The Show Fields dialog box opens.

3. Click the name of the field you want to add in the A̲vailable
   Fields list box. The name you click is highlighted to show
   which field you chose.

4. Click A̲dd. The field you chose is now copied to the bottom of
   the Sh̲ow These Fields in This Order box.

5. Click Move Up to move the field you chose higher on your list.
   Each time you click Move Up, your field moves up one
   position in the list. The highest items on the list are displayed
   closest to the top of any Address Cards view and farthest left
   in any Table view.

6. Click OK to close the Show Fields dialog box. Your new field is
   now displayed in the position you selected.

If the field you want to add doesn't appear in the A̲vailable Fields
list, you may need to choose a different collection of fields from
the box labeled Selec̲t available fields from. The default choice is
Frequently-Used Fields, but you find more choices if you pick a
choice that begins with the word All, such as All Contact Fields, All
Task Fields, and so on. When you do, a much larger selection of
fields appears.

Rearranging views

List-type views, such as the Phone List, can have more columns of
information than fit on the screen. Sometimes placing two columns
together makes them easier to use, such as when you place the
name and phone number columns together.

To move the phone number next to the person's name, follow
these steps:

1. Choose V̲iew➪Current V̲iew➪Phone List to see your phone list.

2. Click the Business Phone heading and drag it on top of the Full
   Name column. The gray heading box containing the words
   Business Phone moves where you drag it.

Contacts - Microsoft Outlook

File Edit View Go Tools Actions Help

Outlook Shortcuts | Contacts

		Full Name	Company	File As	Business Phone	Business Fax
		Click here to add a new C...				
		Snarfus Babbit	Bogwamp Boats	Babbit, Snarfus	(212) 555-8599	
		Henry Beecher	Eggs Etc.	Beecher, Henry	(212) 555-6450	(212) 555-9189
		Vera Blunt	Deuce Hardware	Blunt, Vera	(212) 555-7384	
		Jack D. Carr	HoistCo	Carr, Jack D.	(212) 555-7415	
		Bulah Mae Cheatum	Clemtex	Cheatum, Bulah Mae	(212) 555-1957	(212) 555-7865
		Elmer Coyote	Acme Explosives	Coyote, Elmer	(212) 555-4501	
		Otto B. Early	Eastclox	Early, Otto B.	(212) 555-4203	
		Floyd Fluffernet	Peanut Creations	Fluffernet, Floyd	(212) 555-8561	(212) 555-8666
		Moe Fricker	Salt Mines, Inc	Fricker, Moe	(212) 555-0978	
	0	Pearl E. Gates	Celestial Security	Gates, Pearl E.	(212) 555-1823	
		Heilie N. Likely	Sands, Inc	Likely, Heilie N.	(212) 555-3620	
		Margaret Madd	Clemtex	Madd, Margaret	(212) 555-1952	(212) 555-7865
		Willie Makit	Clemtex	Makit, Willie	(212) 555-1958	(212) 555-7865
		Tuesday March II	Clemtex	March, Tuesday	(212) 555-1959	(212) 555-7865
		Stan Spotman	Megacorp, Inc.	Spotman, Stan	(312) 555-9730	
		Magnolia Thunderblossom	Xemnexx	Thunderblossom, Magnolia	(212) 555-1342	
		Targus Toadslinger	Warts 'n All	Toadslinger, Targus	(212) 555-1484	
		Wanda Woowoo	Psychic Waterbeds	Woowoo, Wanda	(212) 555-7708	

Outlook Today, Inbox, Calendar, Contacts, Tasks, Journal

My Shortcuts
Other Shortcuts

20 Items

3. Release the mouse button.

As you drag the heading across the screen, you see two red arrows moving along the row of remaining column headings. When you release the mouse button, the heading you dragged (in this case, the Business Phone heading) drops into the row of headings specifically in the spot where the arrows point.

Saving and deleting created views

You can save any view you create and use it over and over. To create and save a view, follow these steps:

1. Create a custom view by dragging any column head to a new location or to the Group By box. Your list appears as a grouped view.

2. Choose View⇨Current View⇨Define Views to open the Define Views dialog box.

3. Click Copy to open the Copy View dialog box.

4. Type the name that you want to give your new view under Name of New View (what else?).

5. Click OK to close the Copy View dialog box. (Leave the rest of the settings alone for the moment.) The name you gave to your new view now appears in the list of views for this folder.

6. Click Close to close the Define Views dialog box.

The name of any view you create and save appears in the Current View menu. You can use the view you create any time, just like you use any other view.

If you change your mind or just don't need to use that view anymore, you can easily delete any view that you created and saved.

To delete a created view, follow these steps:

1. Choose View➪Current View➪Define Views. The Define Views dialog box appears.

2. Click the name of the view that you want to delete and then click the Delete button. A dialog box appears, asking Are you sure?.

3. If you're sure, click OK.

4. Click Close.

The Delete button appears only when you click the name of a view that you created. If you try to delete a view that's built in to Outlook, such as the Phone List view, the Delete button doesn't appear, preventing you from accidentally deleting something you shouldn't.

Sorting a view the quick, simple way

Certain views of your Contact list are more useful when you organize the items according to a single piece of information, such as the contact's last name, company affiliation, city, or state.

Some views, such as the Phone List view, can be sorted quickly by clicking the heading of any column that you want to sort. For example, you can sort your Phone List according to the company for which each person in your Contact list works.

To sort your Phone List by the contact's company, follow these steps:

1. Choose View⇨Current View⇨Phone List to show your phone list.

2. Click the head of the Company column to reorder the whole list according to the name of each contact's company.

You can sort any list by clicking any column heading in an Outlook view except Category. Remember, though, you can use only the quick, simple method to sort a view that looks like a list (a Table view, in Outlook-speak). Other views, such as the Address Cards views, don't have column headings that you can click to make the list sort itself. In those cases, you have to use the slow, complete way to sort, which is next.

Sorting a view the slow, complete way

The quick, simple method of sorting your views works only in list views. Views such as the Address Cards view require a different method of sorting that takes more time. Nor does the quick, simple method work when sorting a list by a piece of information that's not showing on the list. For example, the Phone List normally doesn't show the state in which each contact lives, so you can't do a quick sort of the Phone List by state.

Each piece of information that you enter about a contact is called a *field*. Each field shows up as a separate column in the Phone List view. However, each field shows up as a separate *line* in the Address Cards view. When you use the slow, complete method of sorting your Contact list (or sorting the items in any Outlook module), the Sort dialog box refers to each item as a field, that is, the Name field, the State field, and so on.

The slow, complete method takes a little more time, but gives you more choices.

To sort a view according to each contact's state, follow these steps:

1. Choose View⇨Current View⇨Edit Current View to open the View Summary dialog box.

2. Click the Sort button to open the Sort dialog box.

3. Click the scroll-down menu under Sort Items By and choose State from the menu. The word State appears in the Sort Items By box.

4. Click Ascending if you want your view to begin with contacts from states that begin with the letter A, like Alabama and Alaska. Click Descending if you want your view organized in reverse alphabetical order, starting with Wyoming and West Virginia. A black spot appears in the circle next to whichever choice you click.

5. Click OK to begin sorting your list.

6. Choose Yes if a dialog box appears saying `The field "state" that you want to sort by is not shown in the view. Do you want to show it?`. (Frankly, whether you choose Yes or No in this dialog box doesn't matter much; however, don't pick Cancel or Outlook won't sort the list.)

Sometimes you still can't see the field you added, even after you click Yes to the question about showing the field. In views like the Phone List, Outlook adds the new field at the far-right end of the list, so you have to scroll way over to see it. If you want to rearrange the list so that you easily can see the newly added field, *see* "Rearranging views" earlier in this part.

When you open the Sort dialog box, you see four nearly identical boxes. These boxes enable you to choose up to four fields when sorting your view. Outlook sorts the view according to which fields you choose in the order in which you choose them.

Using grouped views

The names of many Outlook views begin with the word *By*, which means that they are grouped views. The Contacts module has three grouped views: By Category, By Company, and By Location. A grouped view clumps the items in the view into groups that have the same piece of information in a certain field. For example, the By Company field clumps together all the contacts from each company.

Each group in a grouped view is represented by a gray bar that has a plus or minus sign at the left side. A plus icon tells you that you have more to see in the group. Just click the plus sign to open the group and see which contacts belong to that group. A minus sign means that the total group is open; you're seeing all there is to see.

Using your own groups with the Group By box

If the grouped views that come with Outlook aren't enough for you, you can always create your own grouped views by using the Group By box.

To create your own grouped views, follow these steps:

1. Choose View⇔Toolbars⇔Advanced to open the Advanced toolbar. You may want to leave the Advanced toolbar open all the time to take advantage of its wider selection of tools. Some folks become confused when faced with too many tools, so they leave the Advanced toolbar off most of the time.

2. Click the Group By box tool on the Advanced toolbar to open the Group By box. The Group By box appears just above the column headings and contains the words Drag a column header here to group by that column.

3. Drag a column header to the gray box to group by that column. (You probably figured that out without my help.) The list now appears as a grouped view, with each group of items separated by a gray bar that describes the group (*see* the earlier section "Using grouped views").

If you change your mind and want to group by a different column, simply drag the header back to the header row you got it from and then drag another header up to the Group By box. You can even drag two or more headers up to the Group By box to create groups within groups.

Beware: The order in which you add multiple headers to the Group By box makes a big difference in how the items are grouped. If you decide to group by City and State, for example, it makes more sense to group by State first and then by City, because states contain cities, so your State groups automatically should contain City groups. Confused? Just give it a try. Anything you can drag into the Group By box can be dragged back to where it came from, so you can't do any harm.

Printing Contact Lists

You can print your Contact lists in a variety of styles. The two basic types of views available in the Contact list — Address Cards and Table — each come out in their own style when you print them.

Printing Address Cards views

When you're viewing the Contacts module from the Address Cards view or the Detailed Address Cards view, you can choose from several print styles. These styles organize the contact information you print the same way it's organized on the screen, as a series of boxes, each containing information about one contact.

To print address cards, follow these steps:

1. Choose View⊅Current View⊅Address Cards to switch to that view.

2. Click the Print tool in the toolbar (or press Ctrl+P) to open the Print dialog box.

3. Choose the style you want from the Print Style list:

• *Card Style* prints your contacts in a style that looks a lot like the Address Cards you see on the screen.

• *Small Booklet Style* prints your Contact list in Address Cards, but arranges the cards in a way that enables you to cut up the pages and staple them together to form a pocket-sized address directory.

• *Medium Booklet Style* is just like Small Booklet Style except that it creates a larger booklet.

• *Memo Style* prints only contacts you've selected by clicking with your mouse before clicking the Print tool. All the information you've entered about the contact appears in a style that looks like a business memorandum.

• *Phone Directory Style* prints in alphabetical order only the names and phone numbers of your contacts.

a

Apple, Bob .... Bus (212) 555-9076

b

Blunt, Vera .... Bus (212) 555-7384

c

Cheatum, Bulah Mae .... Bus (212) 555-1957
                                                        Home (798) 555-8974
                                                        Bus Fax (212) 555-7865

d

Dickory, Hickory .... Bus (212) 555-2342
                                                        Bus Fax (212) 555-7865

e

Early, Otto B. .... Bus (212) 555-4203

f

Flowers, Fern .... Bus (212) 555-3651

Fricker, Moe .... Bus (212) 555-0978
                                                        Home (212) 555-1143

4. Click OK to send your list to the printer.

If you want to select more than one contact in order to print multiple contacts in Memo Style, hold down the Ctrl key while clicking each contact that you want to include.

Printing from Table views

Printing lists of your contacts from Table-style views, such as the Phone List view or the By Company view, enables you to take advantage of the grouping and sorting tricks you can do in Outlook views.

When you print from a Table view, remember: WYSIWYG! What you see is what you get. If you click the Print tool while viewing the By Category view, the By Category view is what you print.

To print from a Table view, follow these steps:

1. Choose a Table-style view, such as Phone List or By Company.

2. Click the Print tool in the toolbar (or press Ctrl+P) to open the Print dialog box.

3. Choose the style you want from the Print Style list:

- *Table Style* prints exactly what you see on the screen.

- *Memo Style* prints only contacts you've selected by clicking with your mouse before clicking the Print tool. All the information you've entered about the contact appears in a style that looks like a business memorandum.

- *Phone Directory Style* prints in alphabetical order only the names and addresses of your contacts.

4. Click OK to start printing your list.

You do the same things to print from Outlook that you do to print from any Windows program: Just put what you want to print on the screen and then click the Print tool.

Part VI

Notes and Journal

The Notes and Journal modules are the modules I use
least. But I find both modules mighty handy when I do
go to them. Notes enables you to keep quick, bite-
sized nuggets of information that are too important to
forget, but not important enough to open your word
processor to write home about.

The Journal can do most of its work for you invisibly.
After you set up Outlook to make Journal entries of
your documents, tasks, and contacts, you deal with
the Journal only when you want to look at the things
the Journal recorded. The Journal keeps a record of
the things you've done.

In this part . . .

✔ Creating and using Notes

✔ Printing and viewing Notes

✔ Creating and using Journal entries

✔ Printing and viewing Journal entries

Notes

Nothing is easier to use than those yellow sticky notes, which is probably why you see them everywhere. I like to stick those little yellow scraps of paper just about anywhere. But, quick as a wink, I forget where I stuck them. Outlook notes are just as easy to use and they're much easier to find.

Creating notes

If you can click a mouse, you can create a new note.

1. If you're not already in the Notes module, click the Notes icon in the Outlook Bar.

2. Click the New Note icon on the toolbar (or press Ctrl+N). A blank note appears.

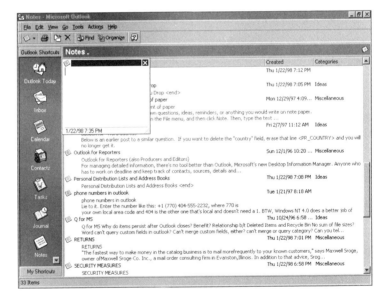

3. Enter what you want to say in your note.

4. Press Esc to close and save the note.

Your new note takes its place in the collection of notes in the Notes module. Creating a note doesn't involve a lot of fuss; just open, type, and close.

To create a note really quickly, you don't even need to switch to the Notes module. Just press Ctrl+Shift+N from any other part of

Outlook. A blank note opens, ready for you to fill in. When you've finished writing your note, press Esc to close the note.

Deleting a note

Creating a huge collection of notes is so easy to do that someday you'll need to delete some of them. Deleting notes is even easier than creating them — a piece of cake.

To delete notes, follow these steps:

1. If you're not already in the Notes module, click the Notes icon in the Outlook Bar.

2. Click the title of the note that you want to delete. The title is highlighted to show which note you've selected.

 3. Click the Delete button in the toolbar (or press Delete). The note disappears.

 You don't have to limit yourself to deleting one note at a time. You can select a whole bunch of notes by holding down the Ctrl key while clicking the different notes you want to delete; then click the Delete button. You also can click one note, and then hold down the Shift key and click another note farther down the row to select both notes you clicked — as well as all the notes in between. When you click the Delete key, all the notes you selected are deleted.

Designating categories for your Notes

You can assign a category to any Note you create in Outlook. Categories may be a bit more useful when you're using Notes than in other parts of Outlook, because you can enter any old kind of information in a note, which can make it hard to find later. Assigning categories makes the stuff you collect easier to use and understand.

To assign a category to a note, follow these steps:

1. Click the Note icon in the upper-left corner of the Note. The shortcut menu appears.

2. Choose Categories. The Categories dialog box appears.

3. Choose one of the existing categories, if one suits you; then click OK.

4. If none of the existing categories suits you, enter a category of your choice in the New Category box.

5. Click OK. Your note looks the same, but now it has a category.

I prefer to choose categories from the Category list rather than type in my own, because using the listed categories keeps your organization consistent, and the list is easy to use. For example, I never remember whether I called the category I created *References* or if I just named it *Refs.* I mean the same thing in both cases, but to a computer, those are two totally different categories. And if I sometimes file names under *Refs* and at other times under *References,* I don't have all my important reference contacts available in one place when I need them.

Editing or reading a note

I normally write notes because I plan to read them later as reminders. Also, I may need to edit them if the information changes. Opening a note so that you can read it or edit it is simple.

To open a note, follow these steps:

1. If you're not already in the Notes module, click the Notes icon in the Outlook Bar.

2. Double-click the title of the note that you want to open. It opens! You see the note on your screen.

3. Read the note or make changes as you want.

4. Press Esc to close the note.

If the note you want to read or edit doesn't appear on the screen when you go to the Notes module, *see* "Finding a note."

Finding a note

After you see how easily you can create a note, you're likely to add notes at the slightest whim, quickly amassing a large collection of notes. Finding one note among a large collection can be a needle-in-a-haystack proposition, except for the Find Items tool. Thank heavens that this tool is easy to use.

To find items with the Find Items tool, follow these steps:

1. If you're not already in the Notes module, click the Notes icon on the Outlook Bar.

2. Click the F̲ind button in the toolbar (or press Alt+I). The Find window opens.

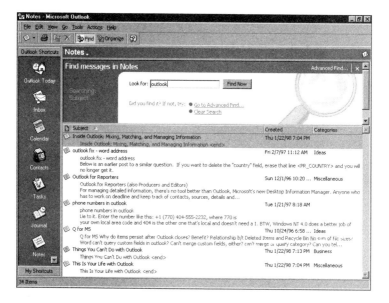

3. In the Look For box, enter the word or phrase you're looking for. It doesn't matter how little text you use for your search. If you're looking for the words *George Washington,* the letters **geo** will find any note that contains the words *George Washing ton.* It will also find *National Geographic* and a reminder to do your geometry homework (assuming you've written notes about all those things).

4. Click the Find Now button. An hourglass appears as Outlook searches for the text you specified. When it's finished, a list of items that satisfy your search appears.

5. If the note you're looking for turns up, double-click the Note icon to read what the note says. If the note you're looking for doesn't show up, try searching on different text.

6. Click the Find button again (or press Alt+I) to close the Find window.

A nice, weird thing about finding notes is that you don't have to enter a whole word. The Find tool can find any sequence of characters that you type. If you're searching for a note you saved about John Paul Kowznofsky, you can search for **John Paul** or just **Kowz.** It doesn't matter whether you use upper- or lowercase letters; Outlook just looks for the letters you entered.

Forwarding a note

After you've accumulated a treasure trove of information in your collection of notes, you don't need to keep these juicy tidbits to yourself. Forwarding a note to anybody by e-mail is simple.

To forward a note by e-mail, follow these steps:

1. Click the title of the note that you want to forward. The title of the note is highlighted.

2. Choose Actions➪Forward (or press Ctrl+F). The New Message form opens.

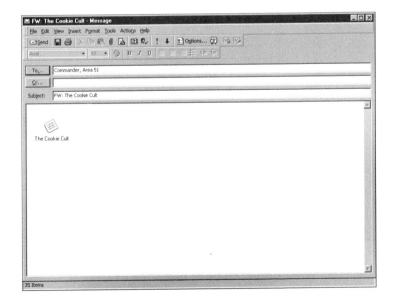

3. Click the To text box and enter the e-mail address of the person to whom you're sending your note. If you want to send a copy to a second person, click the Cc text box and then enter the e-mail addresses of the people to whom you want to send a copy of your note.

4. Enter the subject of the note in the Subject box.

5. If you want, enter the text of a message in the text box.

6. Click the <u>S</u>end button (or press Alt+S). Your message is on the way to your recipient.

What you're really sending is an e-mail message with a note attached, which is very quick and simple, but not terribly magical.

Modifying the size of a note

A note can appear as a teensy little squib, or it can cover your whole screen. The size of the text in the note is the same no matter how large you make the note itself. But when the note is too small, much of your text is invisible. So, you need to make the note larger.

1. Click the Notes icon on the Outlook Bar, if you're not already in the Notes module.

2. Double-click the title of the note whose size you want to change. The note opens.

3. Move your mouse pointer to the bottom-left corner of the note until the mouse pointer changes into a two-headed arrow pointed on a diagonal.

4. Drag your mouse until the note is the size you want.

In most Windows programs, after entering more text than fits in a text box, a scroll bar appears on the right side of the screen. If you want to see text that has scrolled off the bottom of the screen, you click the scroll bar to move the text up. Notes don't have scroll bars, however; so if a note has more text than you can see on the screen, you need to click your mouse on the text and use the arrow keys to scroll up and down through the text. I suppose that those little note boxes are cuter without scroll bars, but they're sure harder to use.

Modifying your note's color

The capability to change the color of a note isn't just an aesthetic option. You can assign various colors to different notes and organize your notes in useful ways. I make notes about things that are going into this book in blue, while I leave all other notes with their normal yellow color.

To assign color to your note, follow these steps:

1. Open the note and click the Note icon in the top-left corner of the note. A shortcut menu appears.

2. Choose C<u>o</u>lor. Another menu appears with a list of colors you can choose.

3. Pick a color. Your note changes to the color you choose.

Choose from <u>B</u>lue, <u>G</u>reen, <u>P</u>ink, Y<u>e</u>llow, or <u>W</u>hite. You can group or sort your notes according to their color (*see also* "Viewing Notes" later in this part).

Printing a list of your notes

Printing lists of the notes you've created is a WYSIWYG process (What You See Is What You Get). Just choose in what view you want to print your notes, and then start printing.

To print a list of notes, follow these steps:

1. Click the Print button in the toolbar (or press Ctrl+P). The Print dialog box opens.

2. Choose Table Style in the Print Style box.

3. Click OK. Your list of notes begins printing.

If you don't want to print all your notes, select the notes you want to print by holding down the Ctrl key and clicking the name of each note you want to print. When you open the Print dialog box, choose Only Selected Rows.

Printing the contents of a single note

Notes are really meant to be read on the screen, but now and then I like to print the contents of a note. Remember, even though you can change the colors of your notes, the colors don't print on a black-and-white printer.

1. Click the title of the note that you want to print. The title of your note is highlighted to show that it was selected.

2. Click the Print button in the toolbar (or press Ctrl+P) to open the Print dialog box.

3. Choose Memo Style in the Print Style box.

4. Click OK. Your note begins printing.

Unfortunately, when you print notes, they don't look like the cute little yellow squares that you see on the screen; each one looks like an office memorandum.

Maybe the next version of Outlook will make the notes that you
print look as cute as the notes that you see on the screen.

Setting the default color and size of your notes

Maybe yellow just isn't your color. Maybe you want a little more
space when you create a new note. You can set up Outlook to start
each note in the color and size that you want (within reason).

To change the default settings for the color and size of your notes,
follow these steps:

1. Choose Tools⇨Options. The Options dialog box opens.

2. Click the Note Options button. The Notes Options dialog box
appears.

3. Click the scroll-down button at the right end of the Color box.

4. Choose a color from the list that appears.

5. Click the scroll-down button at the right end of the Size box.

6. Click OK.

Changing the default size and color of your notes has no effect on the notes you've already created. If you want to change the color of a note after you've created it, just open the note and change the color (*see also* "Modifying your note's color" earlier in this part).

Turning off the date and time display

When you first start Outlook, each note you create includes the time and date that you created the note on the note's bottom line. If that doesn't suit you, you can exclude the time and date information.

To turn off the date and time display, follow these steps:

1. Choose Tools⇨Options. The Options dialog box appears.

2. Click the Other tab to open the Other options page.

3. Click the Advanced Options button to open the Advanced Options dialog box.

4. Click the When Viewing Notes, Show Time and Date check box to remove the check mark.

5. Click OK to close the Advanced Options dialog box.

6. Click OK to close the Options dialog box.

Even if you turn off the time and date display, Outlook displays the time and date of each note's creation in every view except the Icons view (*see also* the following section, "Viewing Notes"). Changing the date and time setting changes only what appears on the little yellow (or blue or green or whatever) square.

Viewing Notes

You can make Outlook display your multitude of notes in a variety of ways. Each type of screen style, called a *view,* emphasizes something different about your collection of notes. You can change between different views of your notes by choosing <u>V</u>iew⇨Current <u>V</u>iew and picking a different view. You can choose from the following views:

✦ *Icons* is a view that splashes your collection of notes in little boxes all over the screen. To open one, just click the box representing the note you want to open.

✦ *Notes List,* as the name suggests, presents a two-column list of your notes. One column is for the subject of each note, and the other column is for the date that you created each note. You can sort the list according to the date you created each note by clicking the word Created in the gray box at the top of the column. You also can sort the list in alphabetical order by subject by clicking the word Subject in the gray box at the top of the column.

◆ *Last Seven Days* view shows only notes you've modified within the last seven days. After more than seven days have passed since you changed either the text in a note or its color, size, or category, the note disappears from the Last Seven Days view, although you see notes of all ages in all other views.

◆ *By Category* groups your notes according to the category you've assigned to each one.

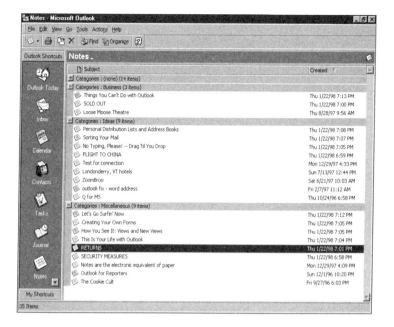

+ *By Color* is a view that groups your notes according to the color you've assigned to each one (*see also* "Modifying your note's color" earlier in this part).

 The AutoPreview button in the Advanced toolbar enables you to see the first few lines of the contents of the items in many Outlook views. You can turn AutoPreview on and off like a light switch, so don't hesitate to click AutoPreview if you want a quick hint of what's in your Notes. AutoPreview is especially useful when you're viewing Notes. Notes are often pretty short, so with AutoPreview, you get a good idea of what your notes are about.

Journal

The Journal is the one part of Outlook that can be useful to you even if you never look at it. If you don't mess with the Journal at all other than to turn the feature on, you still have a record of every document you create, every e-mail message you send and receive, and a chronology of most of your important interactions with the people on your Contact list.

Then again, if you actually use your Journal, you can keep track of meetings, phone calls, conversations, and a number of other routine events. Why would you want all this information? Because sometimes it's hard to remember what you named a document you created or the folder in which you saved a certain spreadsheet. But you *may* remember when you did what you did — like last Thursday. The Journal comes in handy as a chronological record of all your activities.

Activating the automatic recording feature

You wouldn't really be lying if you said that you don't have to do anything to make the Journal work for you. But you'd be exaggerating a little. You do have to tell the Journal to record everything, but you have to tell it only once.

To activate the Journal's automatic recording feature, follow these steps:

1. Choose Tools⇨Options. The Options dialog box opens.

2. Click the Journal Options button to open the Journal Options dialog box.

3. Click to place a check in the check box for those items and files you want to record automatically and for the contacts about whom you want the information recorded.

4. Click OK.

One peculiarity about the Journal is that you can't blithely check off a box that says "Record everything about all my contacts." You must either check off every contact's name in the Journal Options dialog box. Alternatively, you can check the Automatically Record Journal Entries for This Contact checkbox on the Journal tab. This box is in the Contact form when you create each new contact entry. In my humble opinion, this arrangement is silly, but for the moment, you're stuck with it.

Creating Journal entries manually with drag-and-drop

Even though the Cold War is over, you may be skittish about having some computer record all your activities (I think James Bond would've loved the Journal). On the other hand, it's nice to have a record of important things, like phone calls and so on, without exerting too much effort. You can use the manual (drag-and-drop) method to record individual events in your journal.

To record individual events using the drag-and-drop method, follow these steps:

1. Drag the item that you want to record (such as an e-mail message) to the Journal icon. A new Journal Entry form opens.

2. Fill in any information that you want to record.

3. Click Save and Close (or press Alt+S).

Your e-mail message (or whatever you dragged to the Journal icon) is now immortalized in your Journal.

Congratulations!

Creating Journal entries with the New Journal item tool

Drag and drop isn't the only method of creating new Journal entries. You can make a new Journal entry for any reason at all. Simply go to the Journal and create a new item.

To create a new Journal entry, follow these steps:

1. Click the Journal icon in the Outlook Bar, if you're not in the Journal module.

2. Click the New Journal item button in the toolbar. The Journal Entry form opens.

3. Enter the subject of the Journal entry in the Subject text box.

4. Click the scroll-down button on the Entry Type box to pick an entry type.

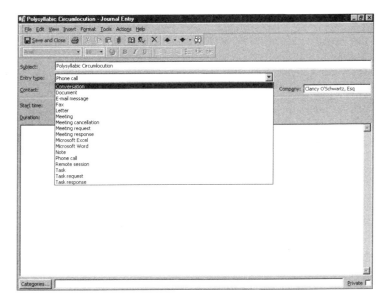

5. If you want to add any other information to the Journal entry, enter it in the appropriate text box.

6. Click <u>S</u>ave and Close (or press Alt+S). Your new Journal entry now appears in your Journal.

You can't easily add Journal entry types the way you can add new Categories (but you can assign categories to Journal entries). For example, if you are frequently served with legal papers, you may want to make an entry type called "Documents Served" or something similar. But that's fairly difficult to do. (Okay, actually you *can* edit the Windows Registry to add Journal entry types, — but hoo-boy! — I wouldn't recommend getting into that!) You can just make a Journal entry for a letter and put it in a category of your choice, the same way you would for any Outlook item (**see** "Designating categories for your Notes" earlier in this part).

Finding a Journal entry

Although the Journal is time-oriented (it tracks items by time and date), occasionally you may need to find a Journal entry without knowing when the entry was made. To dig up the Journal entry you want, simply use the Find Items tool.

To find a Journal entry, follow these steps:

1. Click the Journal icon. Your list of Journal entries appears.

2. Click the F̲ind button in the toolbar (or press Alt+I). The Find window opens.

3. Enter a word or phrase that you can find in your Journal in the Look For text box.

4. If the Journal entry you're looking for turns up, double-click the icon next to the entry to see the item's contents. If the entry you're looking for doesn't show up, try searching on different text.

5. Click the F̲ind button again (or press Alt+I) to close the Find window.

The icon that appears in the text box of your Journal entry is a shortcut to the document itself. You can open the document by double-clicking the shortcut.

Printing your Journal

If you're like me, you just don't get the same picture from a screen that you do from a good ol' piece of paper. It's a good thing you can print out the Journal.

To print your Journal, follow these steps:

1. Click the Journal icon in the Outlook Bar. Your list of Journal entries appears.

2. Choose the view in which you want to print from the Current View menu on the toolbar.

3. Select the entries that you want to print (unless you want to print them all).

Beware! The Journal can record nearly everything you do on your computer, so a Journal list can be very long.

4. Click the Print tool on the toolbar (or press Ctrl+P). The Print dialog box opens.

5. Choose Table or Memo format.

6. Choose All Rows or Only Selected Rows.

7. Click OK to print your Journal entries.

🗋	0	Entry Type	Subject	Start	Duration	Contact	Categories
	W	Microsoft Word	C:\Outlook QuickRef\otqr06.doc	Mon 2/17/97 11:1...	22 minutes	Bill Dyssel	
	W	Microsoft Word	C:\Outlook QuickRef\otqr06.doc	Mon 2/17/97 10:2...	34 minutes	Bill Dyssel	
	W	Microsoft Excel	C:\My Documents\Journal test.xls	Mon 2/17/97 10:1...	14 minutes		
	W	Microsoft Word	C:\Outlook QuickRef\otqr06.doc	Sun 2/16/97 10:1...	85 minutes	Bill Dyssel	
	W	Document	Autoexec.bak	Sun 2/16/97 9:23 ...	0 hours		
	W	Microsoft Word	C:\Outlook QuickRef\otqr06.doc	Sun 2/16/97 2:43 ...	7.5 hours	Bill Dyssel	
	W	Microsoft Word	C:\Outlook QuickRef\otqr06.doc	Sun 2/16/97 1:59 ...	42 minutes	Bill Dyssel	
	W	Microsoft Word	C:\Outlook QuickRef\otqr07.doc	Sat 2/15/97 3:40 PM	22.3 hours	Bill Dyssel	
	W	Microsoft Word	A:\0l21bd.doc	Sat 2/15/97 3:38 PM	3 minutes	Kathy Cox	
	W	Microsoft Word	C:\Outlook for Dummies\Submitted\OU...	Sat 2/15/97 3:35 PM	0 hours	Kathy Cox	
	W	Microsoft Word	C:\Outlook for Dummies\Submitted\Cha...	Sat 2/15/97 3:34 PM	7 minutes	William Dyssel	
	W	Microsoft Word	C:\Outlook for Dummies\Submitted\Cha...	Sat 2/15/97 3:29 PM	1 minute	William Dyssel	
	W	Microsoft Word	C:\Outlook for Dummies\Submitted\OU...	Sat 2/15/97 3:28 PM	1 minute	Kathy Cox	
	W	Microsoft Word	C:\Outlook QuickRef\otqr06.doc	Sat 2/15/97 1:24 PM	76 minutes	Bill Dyssel	
	W	Microsoft Word	C:\Outlook QuickRef\Outlook Procedure...	Sat 2/15/97 1:17 PM	0.1 days	Bill Dyssel	
	W	Microsoft Word	C:\Outlook QuickRef\Part I toc.doc	Fri 2/14/97 4:10 PM	35 minutes	Bill Dyssel	
	W	Microsoft Word	C:\Outlook QuickRef\Outlook Procedure...	Fri 2/14/97 4:09 PM	36 minutes	Bill Dyssel	
	W	Microsoft Word	C:\Outlook QuickRef\OTQR02KC.DOC	Fri 2/14/97 3:27 PM	4 minutes	Bill Dyssel	
	W	Microsoft Word	C:\Outlook QuickRef\Otqr Toc.doc	Fri 2/14/97 3:23 PM	8 minutes	Bill Dyssel	
	W	Microsoft Word	C:\Outlook QuickRef\OTQR03.doc	Fri 2/14/97 3:22 PM	1 minute	Bill Dyssel	
	W	Microsoft Word	C:\Outlook QuickRef\OTQR04.doc	Fri 2/14/97 3:22 PM	2 minutes	Bill Dyssel	
	W	Microsoft Word	C:\Outlook QuickRef\otqr05.doc	Fri 2/14/97 3:22 PM	3 minutes	Kathy Cox	
	W	Microsoft Word	C:\Outlook QuickRef\otqr05.doc	Fri 2/14/97 1:13 PM	3 minutes	Kathy Cox	
	W	Microsoft Word	C:\Outlook QuickRef\otqr05.doc	Fri 2/14/97 11:08 ...	66 minutes	Kathy Cox	
	W	Microsoft Word	C:\Outlook QuickRef\otqr05.doc	Thu 2/13/97 7:02 ...	251 minutes	Kathy Cox	
	W	Microsoft Word	C:\Outlook QuickRef\otqr05.doc	Thu 2/13/97 12:1...	127 minutes	Kathy Cox	
	W	Microsoft Word	C:\Outlook QuickRef\otqr05.doc	Thu 2/13/97 10:1...	97 minutes	Kathy Cox	
	W	Microsoft Word	C:\Outlook QuickRef\otqr05.doc	Thu 2/13/97 10:0...	0 hours	Kathy Cox	Ideas
	W	Microsoft Word	C:\Outlook QuickRef\OTQR04.doc	Wed 2/12/97 11:0...	31 minutes	Bill Dyssel	
	W	Microsoft Word	C:\Outlook QuickRef\OTQR03.doc	Wed 2/12/97 9:44...	111 minutes	Bill Dyssel	
	W	Microsoft Word	C:\Outlook QuickRef\OTQR03.doc	Wed 2/12/97 9:41...	0 hours	Bill Dyssel	
	W	Microsoft Word	C:\Outlook QuickRef\OTQR04.doc	Wed 2/12/97 9:38...	3 minutes	Bill Dyssel	
	W	Microsoft Word	C:\Outlook QuickRef\OTQR03.doc	Wed 2/12/97 9:26...	15 minutes	Bill Dyssel	
	W	Microsoft Word	C:\Outlook QuickRef\otqr05.doc	Wed 2/12/97 9:15...	140 minutes	Kathy Cox	

Bill Dyssel   1   2/17/97

The Print dialog box has a button named Preview, which enables you to see what you're about to print before you actually commit everything to paper. Because a Journal can quickly develop thousands of entries, you would do well to preview what you print before tying up your printer with a document that could be over a hundred pages long. Your office mates will thank you.

Seeing Journal entries for a contact

Automatic journaling of your interactions with your contacts is one benefit you can get from the Journal.

To see what you gained from the Journal, follow these steps:

1. Click the Contacts icon in the Outlook Bar. The Contact list appears.

2. Double-click the name of the contact that you want to view. The Contact form opens.

3. Click the Journal tab in the Contact form to see Journal entries for that contact.

Remember, though, you have to check Automatically Record Journal Entries for This Contact in order to create the automatic entries you see on this page. Another way to generate journal entries is to use the AutoDial feature in the Contact list and check the box that says Create New Journal Entry When Starting New Call.

Viewing the Journal

You can view your Journal entries in a variety of screen arrangements, called *views*. When you first start Outlook, six views are already set up for you to use with the Journal. You can switch among them by choosing View⇨Current View and picking the name of the view you want. If one view doesn't suit you, switch to another view in the same way.

✦ *By Type* view groups your Journal entries on a timeline according to the type of entry, such as e-mail messages, Excel spreadsheets, Word documents, and so forth. You can scroll forward and back in time to see different slices of your Journal.

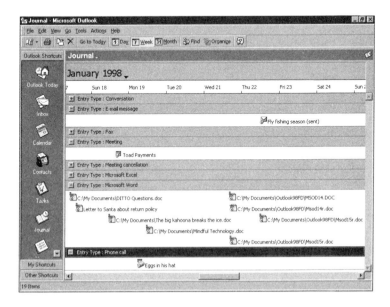

✦ *By Contact* is yet another grouped timeline view that organizes your Journal entries according to the contact associated with each entry. You cannot print the By Contact view of the Journal.

✦ *By Category* looks very much like the By Type view, except that the entries are grouped according to the category you've assigned each entry. You cannot print the By Category view of the Journal.

✦ *Entry List* view is a simple list of all your Journal entries. You can sort the Entry List according to any piece of information listed, such as subject, contact, starting time, or duration. You also can select and copy a range of entries from the Entry List. You then can paste the range into an Excel spreadsheet in order to calculate the total time spent on work for a certain contact or on projects in a certain category.

+ *Last Seven Days* is just like the Entry List but it hides entries that occurred more than seven days ago.

+ *Phone Calls* is a view that shows only the phone calls that you've entered in your Journal.

Viewing a specific date in your Journal

If you use the Journal to record your activities, you accumulate lots of information. Sometimes the amount of information is so great that sorting through all the entries becomes difficult.

To see only the activities on a certain date, here's what to do:

1. Click the Journal icon in the Outlook Bar. The Journal appears.

2. Choose any view that begins with the word *By* (By Type, By Contact, or By Category) by choosing View➪Current View and picking the view you want.

3. Choose Go➪Go to Date (or press Ctrl+G). The Go to Date dialog box opens.

4. In the <u>D</u>ate box, enter the date you want to view, such as
December 16, 1998, or type the amount of time since the date
you have in mind, such as **two weeks ago.**

The display shifts to the date you asked for, and you see a collection of icons representing the Journal entries for the date you
specified. If no entries exist, then no icons appear.

Files and Folders

Keeping track of the files and folders that you create with Office 97 is an important task. The tools that Outlook provides makes keeping track a bit easier. If you've always avoided dealing with files and folders, you may find the whole process less mystifying when you're using Outlook. If you're already a file-management expert, you'll appreciate the new features you get with Outlook.

In this part . . .

- ✓ Basics of files and folders
- ✓ Managing your files
- ✓ Printing and viewing files

About the Outlook 98 File Management Option

Although the file management tools are one of my favorite parts of Outlook, Microsoft decided to make that part of Outlook optional in Outlook 98. If the person who installed your copy of Outlook didn't choose to install the Integrated File Management tools, you won't see the stuff I discuss in this part. (Look for all these tools under the My Computer icon in the Other Shortcuts section of the Outlook Bar.) If you don't have these tools but you want them, insert your Outlook 98 CD-ROM in your CD-ROM drive and follow the prompts for installing the feature called Integrated File Management.

Basics of Files and Folders

Computer geeks like to use strange terms, like *files* and *folders* and *paths,* to make themselves sound smart, but the ideas are pretty simple. I give you the most basic basics here. If you want more, see *Windows 95 For Dummies* by Andy Rathbone (IDG Books Worldwide, Inc.) for the entire lowdown on computer file-management concepts.

About files, folders, and drives

The basic elements of organization on the computer are files, folders, and drives:

+ *Files* are the things you create with your word processor, spreadsheet, and other programs. Whether you call them Letters to Mom or Monthly Report, both are just files to your computer. Files can have different sizes, measured in K (for kilobytes, or thousands of bytes). The 2-page letter you wrote to Mom is probably a smaller file than the 50-page sales report you create at work.

+ *Folders* are places you create for storing your precious files. Imagine each of the files you create with your word processor as a document, and imagine the folder as the file folder in which you store a group of documents.

+ *Disk drives* are like the filing cabinets in which you store all the files and folders. A diskette, or floppy disk, is like a small filing cabinet, big enough to hold maybe a thousand documents, in or out of folders. Diskette drives are usually called drive A these days. You also have a disk drive built into your computer, usually called drive C, which acts just like your diskette, but it's much bigger — big enough to hold hundreds of thousands of documents and the folders you put them in.

Network drives work just like hard disk drives, but they're not actually built into your computer. Though they're named similarly — with letters (like drive F, G, or Z) — network drives are located on another computer on the network to which your computer is connected. If you're not connected to a network, you don't have any network drives.

Looking at drives

You can see your whole collection of disk drives and the files that fill them through the My Computer module in Outlook if you've installed the Outlook 98 File Management Tools. You also have a My Computer icon on your Windows 95 Desktop. You can look at your collection of files and folders in a greater variety of views by using Outlook than by using the regular Windows My Computer icon.

To survey your collection of drives, click the Other Shortcuts group in the Outlook Bar and then click the My Computer icon. The Outlook screen shows a list of all the disk drives available to you. If your computer is connected to a network, a list of all the available network drives appears. If you're using a stand-alone computer, you see only the drives on your own computer, probably diskette drive A and the hard drive, drive C.

Looking at folder lists

Disk drives, especially hard drives and network drives, are normally chock-full of folders. Folders seem like a distraction at first, but they're really a big help. Imagine a filing cabinet big enough to hold 10,000 documents filled to the brim with no file folders to help organize the contents of the cabinet. No one could ever find anything in a mess like that. A nice, neat collection of file folders makes the biggest collection of files easier to use.

To see the folders you have, follow these steps:

1. Click the My Computer icon on the Outlook Bar. A list of your disk drives appears on the screen.

2. Double-click the icon for drive C (or whatever drive you want to view) to reveal the list of folders on the drive.

Remember, if you click the icon for the diskette drive, drive A, you need to be sure that a diskette is in the drive. If you ask your computer to show you the contents of a disk that isn't there, you can expect a very long pause followed by an error message saying `The drive is not ready.`

Also remember that you can have folders inside folders. If you're looking for a specific folder on your disk drive, it may be inside another folder. If at first you don't see the folder you're seeking, open the folder that you think contains your folder by double-clicking the first folder's icon. The list of items in the folder you opened includes folders that are inside your first folder. (Got that? I think I get an F for that explanation.)

Looking at lists of your files

Files contain the nitty-gritty, nuts-and-bolts information that you use. Every document that you create is stored as a file somewhere in your computer. Office 97 likes to send all the files it creates to the My Documents folder, but other programs can send their files wherever they want, so you may have to hunt around to find a file you need.

To look at your files, follow these steps:

1. Click the My Computer icon in the Outlook Bar. A list of your drives appears.

2. Double-click the icon for drive C (or whatever drive you want to view). You see a list of the contents of drive C — a collection of folders and files.

3. Double-click the icon for the My Documents folder (or whatever folder you want to look into). The My Documents folder opens and reveals a list of the files and folders it contains.

Your list of files may show you more information about each file than you really want to know, such as its size, type, the last date the file was modified, and so on. But don't worry; if you're using Outlook to view your files, you can customize the screen to show you as much or little information as you want. You can rearrange views of your files in Outlook exactly the way you can rearrange views of any other group of items (*see* "Rearranging views" in Part V).

Managing Files and Folders

Every time you start a program on your computer, you create, change, or move a file. After you create enough files, you may need to delete or move older files to make room for the new ones. You also may want to delete some files to reduce clutter on your computer in order to find the files you need more easily. Now and then, you may need to exchange files with other people by e-mail, so you need a good set of tools for finding and dealing with the files you're exchanging. Outlook has all the tools you need for your daily file management tasks.

Choosing files

If you've used any Windows program before, you're used to the idea of selecting — clicking an item with your mouse to tell Windows that you plan to do something to or with that item. After selecting an item, you can cut, copy, format, move, open, rename, or do heaven-knows-what to the item you've selected.

Files work exactly the same way. If you plan to do something to a file, such as move or copy the file, you find the file and click the filename to select it. If you want to do something to several files at once, you have more choices:

> ✦ **To select multiple files, all in a row,** click one file to select that file; then hold down the Shift key and click (called a Shift+click) another file several rows above or below the first file you selected. When you Shift+click the second file, both files you clicked are selected, along with all the files in between.

> ✦ **To select multiple files, not in a row,** click one file to select that file; then hold down the Ctrl key while clicking the other files you want to select. Even if the files you click aren't located next to each other, all the files you Ctrl+click are selected.

Copying and moving files

The main reason you have a My Computer icon in Outlook is to enable you to move or copy files between different folders or drives. When you click the icon for any other Outlook module, you see a list of items in that module; you see your contacts when you click the Contacts icon, for example, and your tasks when you click the Tasks icon. Clicking the My Computer icon shows you files and folders on your computer.

To move a file from one folder to another:

1. Click the My Computer icon on the Outlook Bar. A list of your drives appears.

2. Double-click the icon for drive C (or whatever drive you want to view). You see a list of the contents of that drive — a collection of folders and files.

3. Double-click the icon for the My Documents folder (or whatever folder you want to look into). The My Documents folder opens and reveals a list of the files and folders it contains.

4. Select the file (or files) that you want to move. The files you click are highlighted to show that you've selected them.

5. Drag the file to the folder to which you want it to move.

Dragging a file

If the folder to which you drag the file is on the same drive (such as drive C) as the folder from which you dragged it, the file is moved. If you press and hold down the Ctrl key while dragging the file, the file is *copied*. If you drag the file to a different drive, the file is copied unless you hold down the Shift key while dragging the file; then the file is moved.

Deleting files

Another good reason to go to the My Computer section is to delete files that you don't need anymore. Old, unused files don't wither and mold like leftovers in the fridge, but the disk drive fills up surprisingly quickly, so you need to dump unused files now and then. Fortunately, deleting files is easy.

To delete files, follow these steps:

1. Select the file (or files) that you want to delete. The file is highlighted to show you've selected it.

2. Click the Delete button on the toolbar (or press Delete).

3. When the dialog box appears and asks Are you sure . . ., click Yes. Your file disappears.

If you want to clear out whole bunches of files, select several files at once (***see also*** the section "Choosing files").

Renaming files

You can rename files to help you remember what's in them. If you
previously used DOS or Windows 3.1, you were limited to eight-
character filenames; therefore, you had to name your Annual Sales
Report something like **AnSlsRpt**. With Windows 95, however, you
can use up to 255 characters for filenames. So now you can call the
Annual Sales Report something clever, like **Annual Sales Report.**
Now that it's so easy, you may want to go back and rename all
your files so that they have names that make sense to you.

To rename files, follow these steps:

1. Right-click the name of the file you want to rename to open
the shortcut menu.

2. Choose Rename from the menu to open the Rename dialog
box.

3. Type the new name of the file in the Rename dialog box.

4. Click OK. Your new filename appears.

Before you go hog-wild renaming all your files, remember that
older programs still understand only the old eight-letter scheme. If
you rename a file that you need to use in an older program, you
see names like Annual~1.txt when you try to open the file in the
older program. If you only use programs written after 1996, you
see the long filenames.

Renaming folders

Folders exist to make it easier for you to find your files. Also, some
programs have their own folders all to themselves and keep the
files they create close to home. Folders have names the program
gives them, or names that you give them.

Now and then, you may need to rename a folder. If you keep a
folder named *This Year's Taxes,* someday you may rename the
folder *Last Year's Taxes,* and so forth. (Better yet, include the
actual year, or you may need to have *Year-Before-Last Year's Taxes*
and *Year Before the Year-Before-Last-Year's Taxes* — soon you'll be
awash in years before.)

Here's how to rename a folder:

1. Right-click the name of the folder you want to rename to open the shortcut menu.

2. Choose Rename from the shortcut menu. The Rename dialog box appears.

3. Type the new name of the folder in the Rename dialog box.

4. Click OK. Your new folder name appears.

Don't rename the following two folders: *My Documents* is the folder where most Windows programs look to find the documents you've created. Although you can tell your programs to look elsewhere, why go to the trouble? Your *Windows* folder also is very important; if you rename the Windows folder, your computer probably won't start. So leave it alone.

Printing and Viewing Files and Folders

You can use Outlook to print or view lists of the names of all your files, along with details about each file, such as the age of each file, its size, and the name of the program that created the file. If you have a program called QuickView installed, you also can print or view the contents of any file. QuickView is included with Windows 95, but it isn't installed unless you make a point of it.

See *Windows 95 For Dummies* by Andy Rathbone (IDG Books Worldwide, Inc.) for more about QuickView.

About views

In all the other modules of Outlook, you view *items*. Items are just small units of information that Outlook uses to organize all the stuff you enter every day. To some extent, Outlook items are figments of Outlook's imagination; no other program can see Outlook items. When you go over to the My Computer module, you're dealing with files — the actual units of information that other programs have created. Outlook shows you the files created by Word, Excel, and any other program you use, like Bozo's Clown Drawing program, and anything you may have downloaded from the Internet.

In this section, I use the word *viewing* to mean looking at lists of the names of your files and the details associated with each file (*see also* "About views" in Part V). If you want to view the contents of a file, right-click the name of the file and then choose QuickView from the shortcut menu.

Choosing a view

You can slice and dice lists of information about your files in literally hundreds of different ways when using Outlook. The half-dozen predefined views that come installed when you first use Outlook give you a good selection. You can choose any view of your files by choosing View➪Current View and picking the view you want:

✦ *Icons* view spreads a bunch of icons all over the screen, each representing one file. The icons you see differ, depending on the type of file you're seeing. Files created by Microsoft Word have a different type of icon than files created by Excel, which are different than the icons that represent Quicken files, for example.

✦ *Details* view shows you a simple list of your files by name, along with the size of each file, the last date that you modified the file, and the author of the file (if author information is available).

✦ *By Author* view groups your files according to the author of each file. Not every program you use keeps track of the author of each file, so many files may end up under a group called None.

Office 97 programs track the name of the author of each document; if you only use Office 97 programs, the Author view may be useful to you.

✦ *By File Type* is a view that groups your files according to type, which really means the name of the program that created the file. You then can view only your word-processing files, only your spreadsheet files, or only any other type of file, as you prefer.

✦ *Document Timeline* is a graph of icons, arranged to show when you worked on each document and for how long. The Document Timeline is handy for times when you can recall when you worked on a document but not where you filed the document.

♦ *Programs* view shows program files only — the actual computer programs that do all the work of your computer.

You don't want to delete, move, or rename program files unless you have a really good reason for doing so. The Programs view, however, makes it easier to find program files when you need them.

Copying a list of filenames to use in another program

One file-management trick you can do in Outlook that you can't readily do otherwise is to copy a list of filenames and details and then paste the list into another program, such as Microsoft Word or Excel. Using this technique helps you keep track of the progress of projects that involve the creation of many files. For example, as I write this book, I like to know how many parts are finished, how many illustrations are finished, and so on.

Here's how to copy a list of filenames to use in another program:

1. Open the folder in which you stored the files whose names you want to copy (*see also* the section "Choosing a view"). A list of your files appears.

2. Select the files whose names you want to copy (*see also* "Choosing files" earlier in this part). The files you select are highlighted.

3. Choose Edit⇨Copy (or press Ctrl+C).

4. If the other program is not open, click the Start button and then find and open the program.

5. Choose Edit⇨Paste (or press Ctrl+V) where you want the list to appear. The list of file details appears in the new document.

By pasting a list of file details into a spreadsheet such as Excel, you can calculate total file size, sort the files, or perform any calculation on the information that you pasted.

Formatting columns

Column formatting is the term Outlook uses for the type and amount of information that shows up in any column view, as well as what kind of abbreviations Outlook uses to express the information. The best example of column formatting is the way dates are shown. The date and time that you modify each file is displayed in the Modified field. If you prefer the most complete version of the date, you can have Outlook display the date as `Wednesday, March 4, 1998, 12:15 PM`. If you want the date to look more concise, you can choose to show the date in the shortest way possible, `3/4/98`.

To choose how the date and time appear, follow these steps:

1. Open the shortcut menu by right-clicking the title of the column that you want to format.

2. Choose Format Columns from the shortcut menu. The Format Columns dialog box appears.

3. From the Available Fields list, choose the format that you want to use.

4. Click OK. The column you chose now appears in the format you picked.

Whatever format you choose applies only to the folder you're viewing. If you change the date format for the My Documents folder and then want to do the same in your Favorites folder, you must switch to the Favorites folder and repeat the process. Folder columns keep the formatting you assign to them until you change them.

Printing a list of files

Printing lists of files is another trick that's hard to do without Outlook. You have many reasons to print a list of a folder's files. Again, my favorite reason is to be able to keep track of my progress when I'm working on projects that involve creating lots of files.

Here's how to print a list of files:

1. Open a folder that contains files (see "Looking at lists of your files" earlier in this part).

2. Select a file or group of files that you want to print a list of.

3. Click the Print button in the toolbar (or press Ctrl+P).

4. Choose Table Style from the Print Style list. Table Style prints a list of your files rather than details about just one file.

5. If you want to print a list of only the files that you select, choose Only Selected Rows in the Print Range section.

6. Click OK to start printing your list.

When you click the Print button on the toolbar, Outlook prints the list of your files in whatever view you have on screen. If the view on screen doesn't include the information you need, switch to a view that does.

Name	Author	Size	Modified	Keyw...	Com...
Type : Microsoft Excel Worksheet (4 items)					
Type : Microsoft Word Document (12 items)					
Academy Award Acceptance Spee...	Bonkers McGee	19 KB	Wed 2/19/97 9:19 PM		
Canterbury Tales	Lady Di	19 KB	Wed 2/19/97 9:02 PM		
Farewell Address	Bonkers McGee	19 KB	Wed 2/19/97 8:58 PM		
Gettysburg Address	J. P. Getty	22 KB	Wed 2/19/97 8:59 PM		
Grammy Acceptance Speech	Bonkers McGee	22 KB	Wed 2/19/97 9:20 PM		
Magna Carta	Sarah Ferguson	19 KB	Wed 2/19/97 9:00 PM		
My Last Diet	E. Hirohito	27 KB	Wed 2/19/97 9:04 PM		
Nobel Acceptance Speech	Bonkers McGee	19 KB	Wed 2/19/97 9:20 PM		
North by Northwest	L.L. Bean	19 KB	Wed 2/19/97 9:04 PM		
Romeo & Juliet & Hamlet	Seena Ghost	22 KB	Wed 2/19/97 9:05 PM		
Securities Exchange Act of 1934	I.M. Rich	27 KB	Wed 2/19/97 9:06 PM		
Spectacle in Newark	Don B. Shy	22 KB	Wed 2/19/97 9:06 PM		

Bill Dyssel   1   2/19/97

Rearranging columns

You can move a column to a new location simply by dragging its heading. You use exactly the same process for rearranging columns in a list of files as you use for rearranging columns in any other Outlook module.

To move the size column next to the name of the file, follow these steps:

1. Choose View⇨Current View⇨Details to see your list of files.

2. Click the Size heading and drag it on top of the Name column. The gray heading box containing the word Size moves where you drag it.

3. Release the mouse button.

As you drag the heading across the screen, you see two red arrows moving along the row of remaining column headings. When you release the mouse button, the heading you dragged (in this case, the Size heading) drops into the row of headings specifically in the spot where the arrows point.

Sorting files the quick, simple way

You can sort your list of files exactly the same way that you sort any list of items in other Outlook modules:

To sort files, follow these steps:

1. Choose any view other than Icons view.

2. Click the heading of the column containing the information that you want to use to sort your list, such as Name or Date Modified.

Your list of files appears on screen in order of the type of information in the column you clicked. If you want to reverse the order (smallest to largest, or largest to smallest), click the heading a second time.

Sorting files the slow, complete way

You can use an advanced method of sorting your files that enables you to sort according to more than one piece of information. If you want to see the most recent files by a certain author, for example, you can use the slow, complete way to sort by both criteria:

1. Choose View⇔Current View⇔Edit Current View from the menu. The View Summary dialog box opens.

2. Click the Sort button. The Sort dialog box opens.

3. Click the scroll-down menu on the Select available fields from box and choose All File Fields.

4. Click the scroll-down menu under Sort Items by and choose Author from the menu.

5. Click the scroll-down menu under Then by and choose Modified.

6. Click OK.

Of course, you don't have to limit yourself to the fields I use for my example. You can sort any fields in the list of Sort items that show up in Step 3.

Many of the fields that you can display and use for sorting files can't be filled in through Outlook. Typically, file information can be entered only through the program that created the file. For example, to fill in the Keywords or Category fields for a document you create in Microsoft Word, open the document in Word, choose File⇔Properties and then fill in the Keyword or Category boxes.

Using grouped views

A *grouped view* organizes your list of files or Outlook items into, yes, *groups* of files. Each group is made up of files that have one similar piece of information, such as the same author or the same program that created each file.

The names of many Outlook views begin with the word *By,* which means that they are grouped views. You can view your files By Author and By File Type. A grouped view clumps the items in the view into groups that have the same piece of information in a certain field. For example, the By Author view clumps together all the documents created by a single author.

Each group in a grouped view is represented by a gray bar that has a plus or minus sign at the left side. A plus icon tells you that you have more to see in the group. Just click the plus to open the group and see which items belong to that group. A minus sign means that the total group is open; you're seeing all there is to see.

Quick Tricks

If you spend lots of time managing files — perhaps because people e-mail files to you or you download lots of files from the Internet or online services — you'll be glad to know that Outlook has some quick tricks for making your lists of files easy to view and for easily navigating around your folders.

Get the best fit

If a column in any view is much wider or narrower than the information in the column, just double-click the line in the gray header row that separates that column from the column to the right. The column width changes to the width of the widest piece of information in the column.

Go up one level

If you spend lots of time putting files in folders, you know that, beneath it all, Windows organizes folders *hierarchically*, which means that all folders are related to each other like the branches of a tree. Each twig is connected to a branch, each branch to the trunk; the trunk is connected to the root. If you climb a tree and want to move from one branch to another, one sure way is to move back to the trunk and then to the branch you want. The Go⇨Up One Level command enables you to move back toward the root and then resume your travel toward the branch you want.

Navigate with browser buttons

Lots of people browse the World Wide Web using browsing programs such as Netscape and Internet Explorer. Outlook has commands on the Go menu that enable you to browse your computer. When you switch from one folder to another, the browser buttons light up, telling you that they're ready for your use. Suppose that you're copying files from a diskette to the My Documents folder; you easily can switch back and forth between two folders by choosing Go⇨Back.

Techie Talk

ActiveX

A technology for enabling computer programs to share
information and work with multiple documents at the
same time. Outlook is what techies call an *ActiveX
container,* which means that you can add more
sophisticated features to the product in the future, as
programmers develop things to add. Previously,
ActiveX was called OLE (object linking and embed-
ding), but hearing Bill Gates say OLE all the time made
people think he wanted to be a bullfighter.

Address Book

The section of Outlook that stores names and addresses, especially e-mail addresses, so that you
quickly can get at the e-mail address you want when
you're sending an e-mail message.

Application

A computer program or something that can act like a computer program, responding in various ways to user input.

Appointment

An entry in the Calendar module that is assigned to a specific time and date.

Archive

A collection of old items that are put aside for storage.

Attachment

A file that is linked to an e-mail message or other item in Outlook. When you send an e-mail message with a file attached, the recipient of your message receives a copy of the file you attached.

Categories

Keywords for classifying items in Outlook. All items can be assigned to one or more categories, as well as sorted or grouped according to the category to which they belong.

Contact

An item that includes a person's name, address, and other personal information about that individual, which is stored in the Outlook Contacts module.

Cool

A term that is used entirely too often on the Internet.

Date Navigator

The small calendar that turns up in certain views of the Outlook Calendar module that you can use to quickly change the date you're viewing.

Directory

The name folders used before they went Big Time (Windows rather than DOS). See *folder*.

Disk Drive

The physical device that stores your data. Can be a removable disk (like a diskette drive) or a fixed disk (like a hard drive).

Drag and Drop

A method of moving information within a document or between Outlook modules. To *drag* means to select an object on the screen with the mouse and move the mouse to another area of the screen while holding the mouse button down. To *drop* means to release the mouse button over the part of the screen where you want the object to end up.

E-Mail

A system of sending and receiving electronic messages between computers. Messages can include text, pictures, sounds, or computer programs.

Event

An item in the Outlook Calendar that happens on a particular date or series of dates, but isn't assigned a specific time of the day. Holidays and birthdays are events.

Exchange Server, or Microsoft Exchange Server

A product created by Microsoft to store, transmit, and share messages between groups of computer users. You can use Outlook with Microsoft Exchange Server.

Favorites Folder

A folder that stores all your favorite documents and links to sites on the Internet. Clicking the name of an Internet site in your Favorites folder opens your Web browser and connects you to the designated site.

Field

A single piece of information in an Outlook item. In a Contact item, for example, the person's name is one field, the job title is another field, phone number another, and so on. Each item is made up of several fields, which can be displayed as areas on a form or as columns in a list.

File

A named unit of information on your disk. A document can be a file and so can a computer program or a picture or sound.

Filter

A way to display only items that satisfy certain criteria and hide all other items. For example, you can filter your Task list to show only the tasks that are due in the next seven days and hide the tasks that come due later.

Flag

A setting you can apply to an e-mail message in order to remind yourself to take action on the message at a specific time later. Flagging can also be applied to messages you send to other Outlook users to remind them (that's called nagging).

Folder

A place where you can store files as well as other folders. Formerly known as directories.

Font

A typeface, such as Courier or Times New Roman.

Form

A box of information organized to enable you to enter, read, or edit information about a single item. Every time you open an item in Outlook, you see a form that organizes your data.

Format

The arrangement of words and numbers in a field. Date formats include simple formats, such as *1/23/98,* or more detailed formats, such as *Tuesday, March 3, 1998.*

Group

To organize items into collections that have at least one field containing the same information. To group By Category in Outlook is to gather items together that are assigned to the same category.

Internet

The network of networks; a collection of computer networks that links other computer networks around the world. Includes the World Wide Web, newsgroups, e-mail, and other attractions that can consume most of your time.

ISP

An Internet service provider is a firm that connects individual computers and small networks to the Internet. Many online services, such as CompuServe, also function as Internet service providers.

Journal

The Outlook module that keeps track of your computer's activities and saves information about your activities in a chronological context.

Link

A reference to a file in another file. Linked files can share data or enable the viewer to switch between linked files by using a mouse to click the reference to the link.

Mail Merge

The process of creating a personalized group of letters by combining a single letter with a list of names of the people to whom the letter is to be addressed. When mail-merged letters are sent too often or to the wrong people, they're called junk mail.

Mailbox

The file that stores all items in Microsoft Outlook or Microsoft Exchange Server. You can have more than one mailbox. (There's no actual box; it's just the name of the file.)

My Computer

The name of the folder that contains all the resources available on one computer running Windows 95, including disk drives, folders, network connections, and other devices.

Network

A collection of computers that are connected to talk to each other. Computers on a network can share programs and documents and can exchange e-mail.

Notes

The Outlook module that enables you to input free-form text in the form of colored notes on screen.

PowerPoint

The graphics presentation program that's part of Office 97.

Preview

A short sample of the first few lines of text in a message or other Outlook item.

Properties

The qualities or attributes of a file or other object in Windows 95. The font is a property of a piece of text; the filename is a property of a file.

Recurrence

The pattern by which an appointment or task repeats itself. A recurring appointment happens over and over in a predictable pattern.

Regeneration

The pattern by which a task becomes due again a certain amount of time after it was completed the last time.

Registry

A file in Windows 95 that keeps track of all programs and resources on the machine that runs that particular copy of Windows 95.

Rules Wizard

A program that automatically moves e-mail from certain people to a certain folder, or deletes e-mail with certain words in the subject line. The Rules Wizard also enables you to make certain things happen when certain kinds of messages arrive, such as playing a rude sound when messages arrive that contain the word *taxes,* or making a message pop up on your screen when a high-priority message arrives.

Scroll-Down Button

A triangle at the end of a drop-down list that, when clicked, causes the contents of the list to be revealed so that you can choose an item from the list.

Selecting

Highlighting something so that Windows knows that you want to do something to it, such as copy, print, open, rename, and so on. The easiest way to select something is to click it with your mouse or drag your mouse across it.

Server

One computer on a network that holds programs or files for all the other computers on that network to use.

Shortcut

An icon in Windows 95 that represents a program, folder, or document that is located someplace else on the computer. Shortcuts enable you to open programs and documents without having to worry about where they're actually located on the computer.

Sort

To organize a list in order. You can use Outlook to sort names alphabetically or to sort other items by date or size. Outlook can't sort the socks in the laundry just yet.

Start Button

That handy little button at the bottom of your Windows 95 screen that you use to start programs, open documents, and find things on your computer.

Task

An item of work you need to do that you enter in your Task list so that you'll remember to do it.

Taskbar

The stripe across the very bottom of the Windows 95 screen that shows you what programs are running. The taskbar also includes tidbits like the current time and the Start button.

Template

An item that you use as a pattern for creating other items. You can use templates in Outlook to create e-mail messages that contain information that you use over and over, such as a "While you were out" phone message template.

Timeline

A graph that displays a collection of documents or Outlook items according to the time when you created or scheduled each item.

URL

Uniform Resource Locator, a fancy name for the address of anything on the World Wide Web, such as `http:\\www.dummies. com` or any of the `www.something.com` addresses that have sprouted up everywhere.

View

An arrangement of items in Outlook, which you can save and name for future use. Different views help you do different kinds of work. One view of your Tasks module, for example, shows the tasks that you still need to do so that you can get them done; another view shows the tasks that you've finished so that you can approach your boss for that raise.

Visual Basic

The programming language that enables clever programmers to make Office 97 programs, especially Outlook, do things we haven't thought of yet.

Wizard

A series of dialog boxes that guide you step-by-step through procedures that wouldn't make sense to a normal person without help. Wizards can help you create Inbox rules, get remote e-mail, and create a form letter with mail merge.

Word

The word-processing program that accompanies Outlook in the Office 97 suite. You can use Word 97 to create fancy-looking e-mail and then send the mail with Outlook to impress your friends. You also can include addresses from your Contact list in Word documents.

World Wide Web

A collection of documents and graphics on computers all over the world that you can look at by logging on to the Internet and using a Web browser, such as Netscape Navigator or Microsoft Internet Explorer. Each Web page has an address (see **URL**) that you can enter in any Outlook item.

Index

Microsoft Outlook 98 For Windows For Dummies QR

(continued)

S

W

Notes

Notes

Notes

Notes

Discover Dummies Online!

The Dummies Web Site is your fun and friendly online resource for the latest information about *For Dummies*® books and your favorite topics. The Web site is the place to communicate with us, exchange ideas with other *For Dummies* readers, chat with authors, and have fun!

Ten Fun and Useful Things You Can Do at www.dummies.com

1. Win free *For Dummies* books and more!
2. Register your book and be entered in a prize drawing.
3. Meet your favorite authors through the IDG Books Worldwide Author Chat Series.
4. Exchange helpful information with other *For Dummies* readers.
5. Discover other great *For Dummies* books you must have!
6. Purchase Dummieswear® exclusively from our Web site.
7. Buy *For Dummies* books online.
8. Talk to us. Make comments, ask questions, get answers!
9. Download free software.
10. Find additional useful resources from authors.

Link directly to these ten fun and useful things at http://www.dummies.com/10useful

For other technology titles from IDG Books Worldwide, go to www.idgbooks.com

Not on the Web yet? It's easy to get started with *Dummies 101*®: *The Internet For Windows*® *98* or *The Internet For Dummies*® at local retailers everywhere.

Find other *For Dummies* books on these topics:

Business • Career • Databases • Food & Beverage • Games • Gardening • Graphics • Hardware
Health & Fitness • Internet and the World Wide Web • Networking • Office Suites
Operating Systems • Personal Finance • Pets • Programming • Recreation • Sports
Spreadsheets • Teacher Resources • Test Prep • Word Processing

IDG BOOKS WORLDWIDE
BOOK REGISTRATION

Register This Book and Win!

We want to hear from you!

Visit **http://my2cents.dummies.com** to register this book and tell us how you liked it!

- ✔ Get entered in our monthly prize giveaway.

- ✔ Give us feedback about this book — tell us what you like best, what you like least, or maybe what you'd like to ask the author and us to change!

- ✔ Let us know any other *For Dummies®* topics that interest you.

Your feedback helps us determine what books to publish, tells us what coverage to add as we revise our books, and lets us know whether we're meeting your needs as a *For Dummies* reader. You're our most valuable resource, and what you have to say is important to us!

Not on the Web yet? It's easy to get started with *Dummies 101®: The Internet For Windows® 98* or *The Internet For Dummies®*³ at local retailers everywhere.

Or let us know what you think by sending us a letter at the following address:

For Dummies Book Registration
Dummies Press
10475 Crosspoint Blvd.
Indianapolis, IN 46256

FOR DUMMIES™

BESTSELLING
BOOK SERIES